Emerging Voices

Laurel D. Rund

A bird doesn't sing because it has an Answer.
It sings because it has a Song!

Maya Angelou

Emerging Voices by Laurel D. Rund

Contact: *EssenceofLaurel@me.com*

ISBN-13: 978-0-615-39430-5
Printed in the United States of America

Dedication

This journal is dedicated to Marty, my late husband, with gratitude and love. His unconditional commitment, support and love enabled me to become the woman that I am today. He truly was "the wind beneath my wings."

To our sons, Brian and Matthew ~ who were created from love ~ I am grateful for your being. Our legacy continues to live on through you and your families.

To our grandchildren, Tyler, Jordan, Katie and Ashley ~ thank you for the joy and wonderment you bring forth each day and for reminding me that life always renews itself.

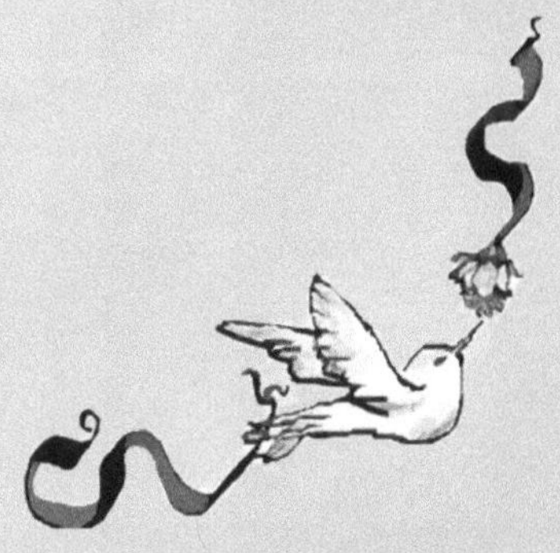

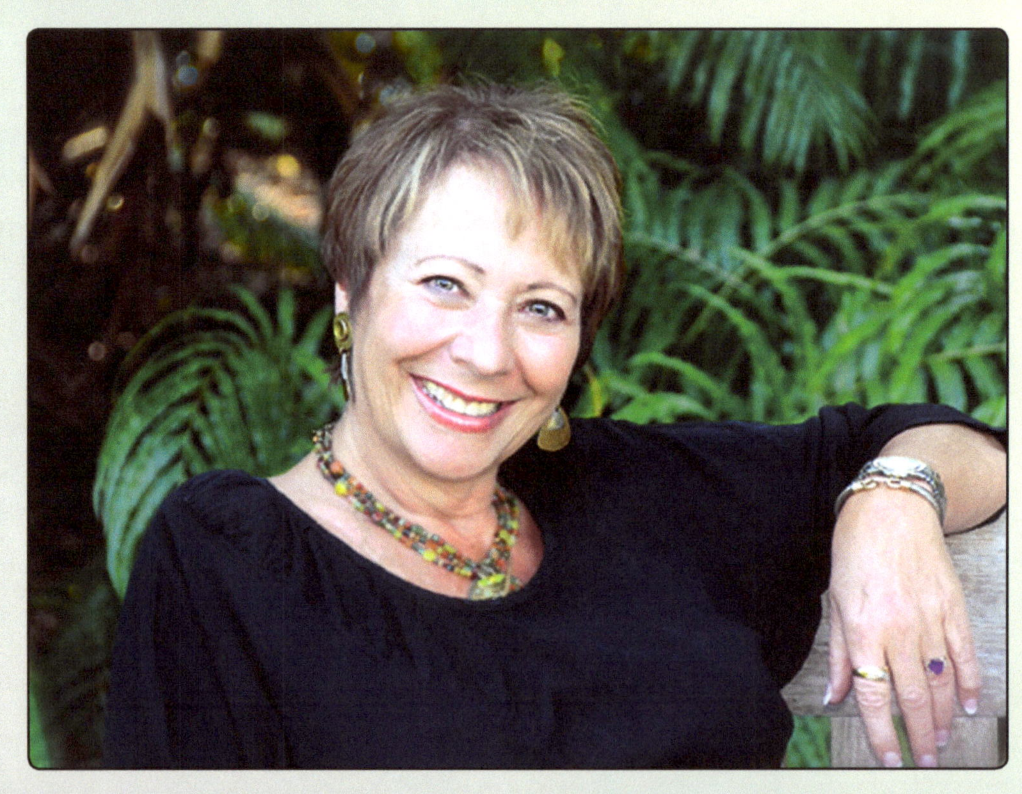

Laurel D. Rund
Inspirational Writer and Artist

Introduction

We have all experienced or will encounter loss and transition in life. It shows up in many faces and forms ~ death, divorce, separation, loss of purpose or value, the transience of time (a precious commodity) and the passing of our youth and/or physicality.

Our human experience, whether in a crisis or a life transition, continuously gives us the opportunity to learn and grow. We can choose to stay in a place of sorrow and regret, or embrace these life-altering experiences from which we can discover a new perspective, sense of understanding and serenity.

My words and art have a purpose ~ to take you on a journey to your heart. As you go inward and your own unique feelings or thoughts surface, experience your Emerging Voice. Embrace your human spirit and ....

Listen to your music ... Find your rhythm ...
Celebrate this dance called Life!

Laurel

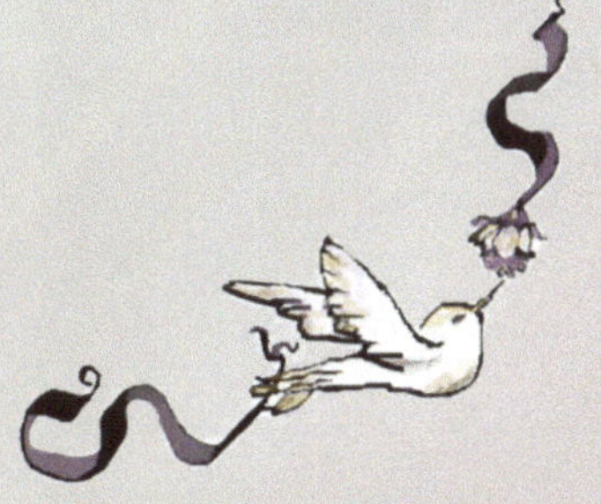

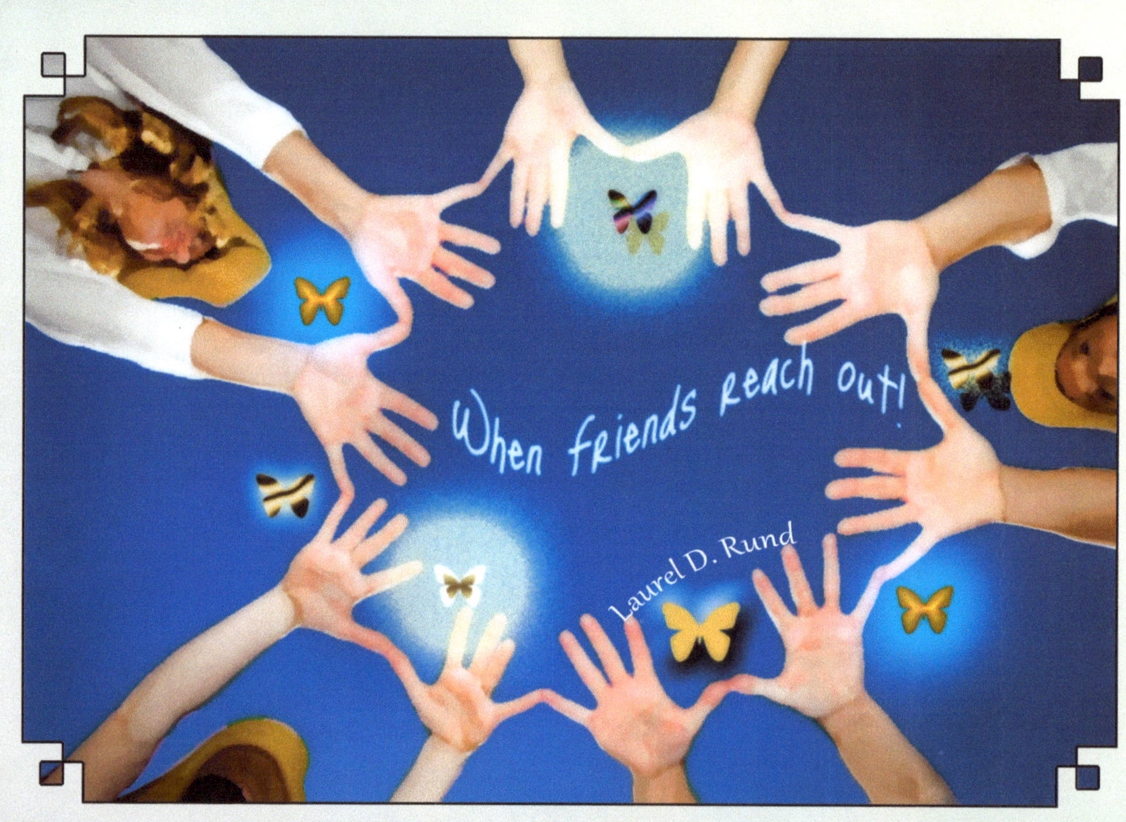
When friends reach out!
Laurel D. Rund

Acknowledgements

I would like to thank my dear friends and family for your love, inspiration and encouragement. You asked me to believe in myself ~ to be courageous ~ to envision and create! Your reassuring voices helped light the way for me, providing a safe haven and confidence that took me on a journey of self-discovery. To each and every one of you, I remain ever grateful!

When Friends Reach Out

When friends reach out, our souls connect.
Something indescribable fills the air as we speak about
our lives, our successes, troubles or fears.
It is about being there for one another
~ picking up where we left off ~
instinctively knowing what to say or do!

The rules are quite simple.
We open our hearts, tell our stories and,
if asked for, give or receive heartfelt counsel.
When we speak of life's challenges ~
understanding and reassurance is offered.
We cheer for each other and revel in delight
when there is a victory!

And, when sharing our visions and dreams,
we encourage each other to go forth
to unearth and embrace our unique potential.

Through the ties of time and shared history,
the circle remains unbroken.
Because you see ~ when friends reach out ~
they are a gift, a cherished treasure!

Laurel

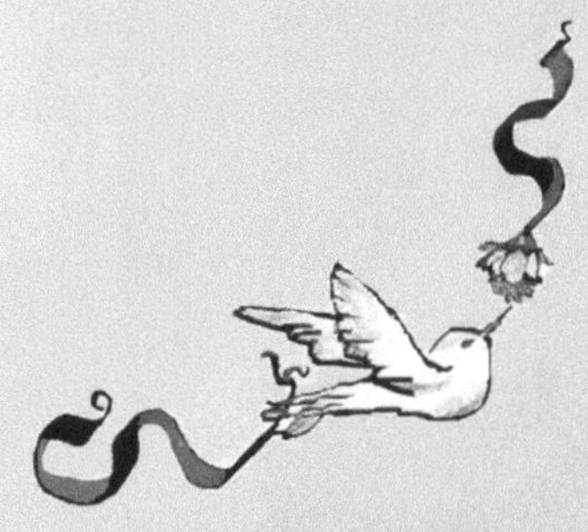

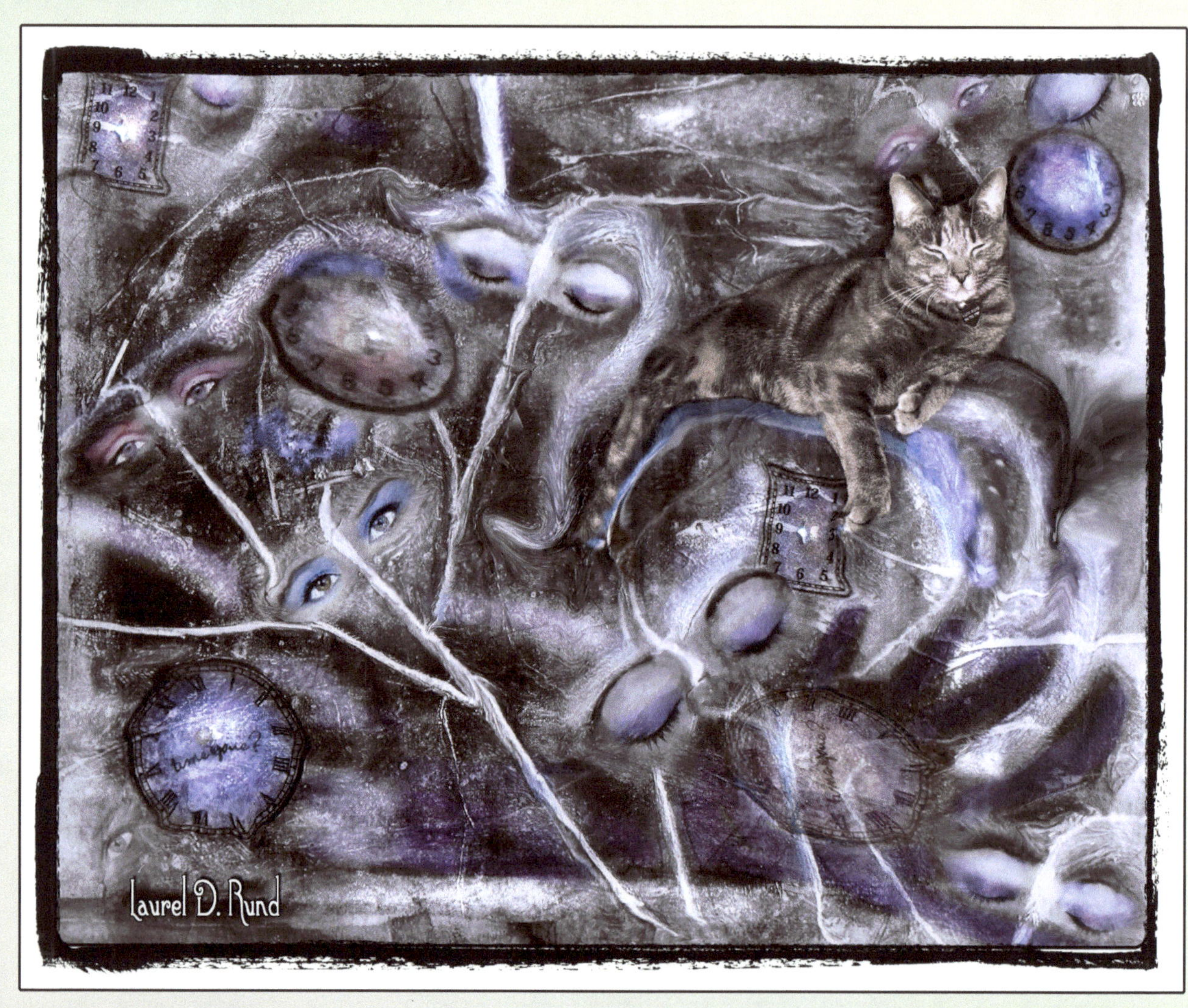

I Blinked My Eyes

I wrote *I Blinked My Eyes* while reflecting about my grown sons and how quickly time had slipped away. Then in 2009, after the death of my husband Marty, this poem took on a deeper and more profound perspective about the passing of time. Even though its essence is one of regret, I have since learned that staying in the present moment is to live life at its fullest. It is really all we have!

I Blinked My Eyes

The wise ones told me not to do it ~
but I was young and foolish.
Challenges surrounded me
and I wished them away, just wished them away.
I blinked my eyes ~ I blinked my eyes
and my life happened!

Thinking things would be better down the road ~
but suddenly it happened.
I blinked my eyes and time melted away.
It just melted away!
Gently, but so swiftly, life unrolled itself ~
time was flying, slipping away,
it was slipping away.

Now, I miss those moments that are lost forever.
Because you see ~ I wished them away,
just wished them away!
And as foretold,
I blinked my eyes ~ I blinked my eyes
and my life happened!

Laurel

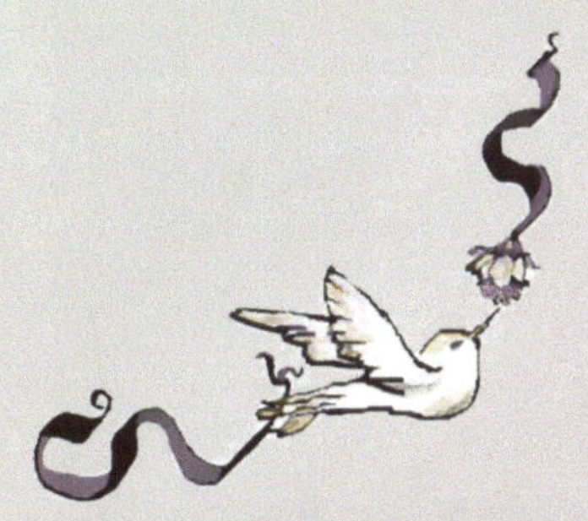

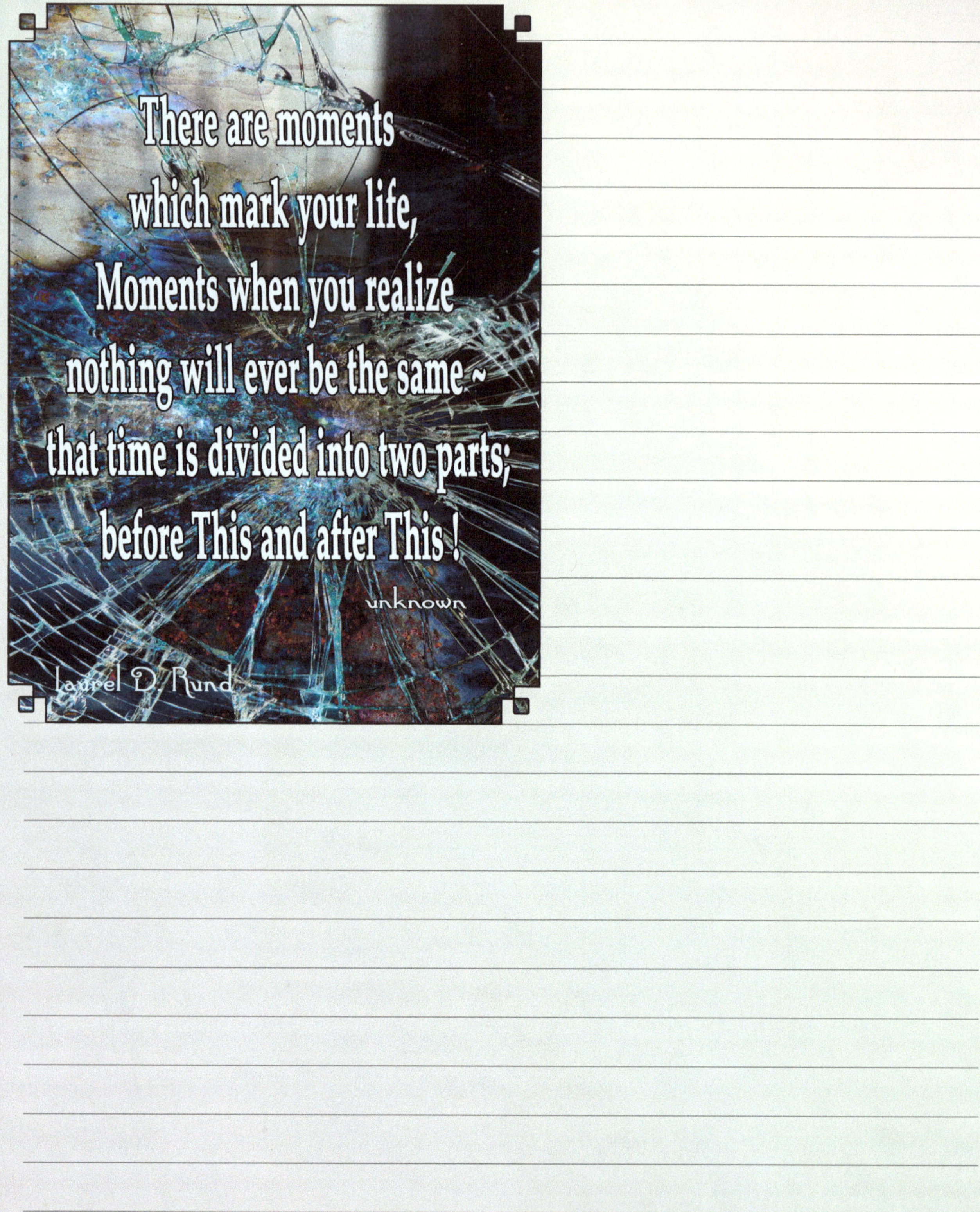
There are moments
which mark your life,
Moments when you realize
nothing will ever be the same ~
that time is divided into two parts;
before This and after This !
unknown
Laurel D. Rund

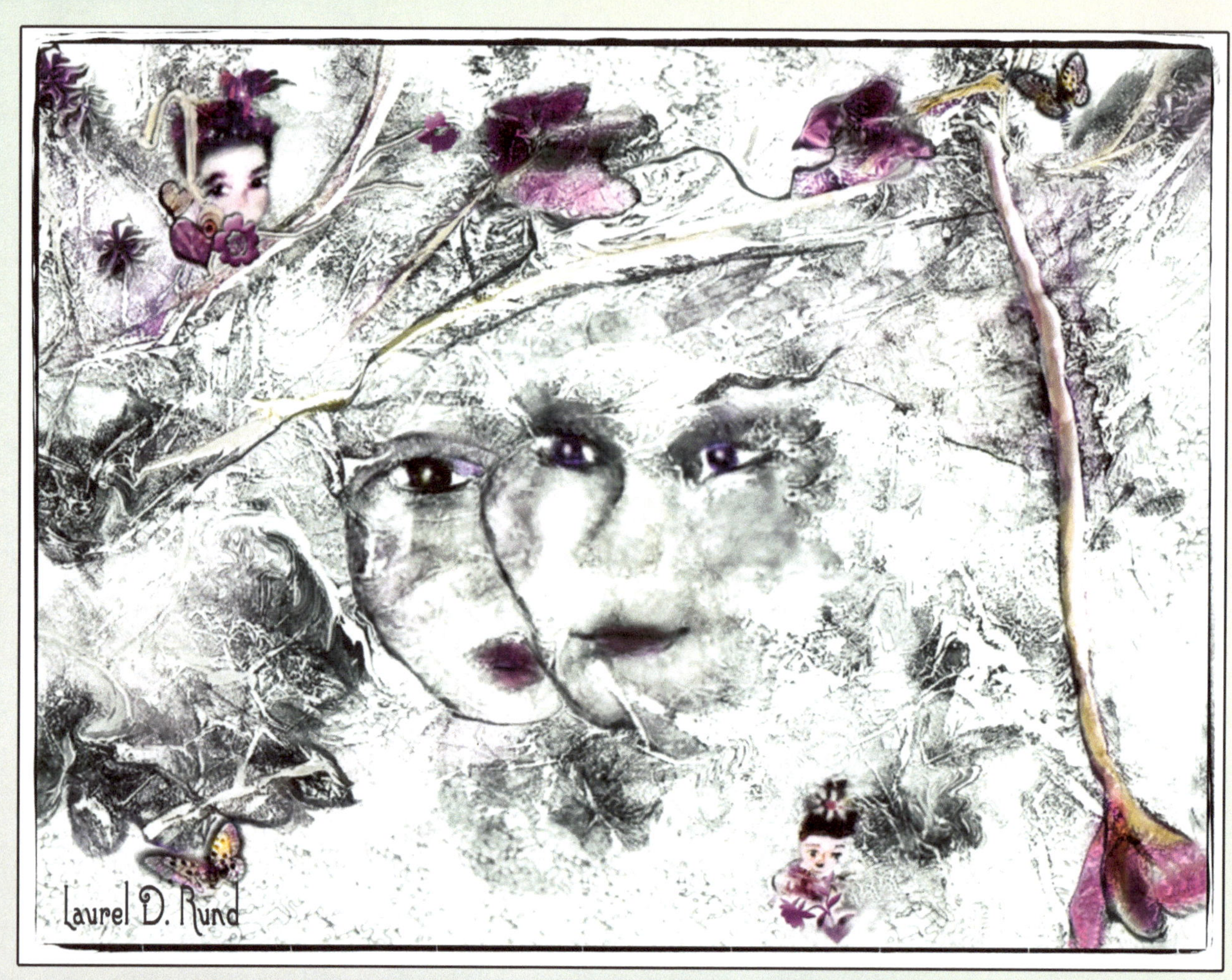

Metamorphosis

Transitions

We were battle scarred and knew the long struggle was about to end.
Simply put, you were dying ~ going to leave.
An acute awareness filled the air; the clock had run out.
Our time together was rapidly coming to an end!
The face of death made itself known to us at warped speed.
It had been lurking around for months ~ playing hide and seek ~
and was finally declaring itself the winner.
Wanting to claim its reward, death beckoned!

Embracing whatever time was left, you became focused and alert.
Your eyes cleared as they sought memories.
As you spoke and wrote to those whom you loved,
you found the courage to say a final goodbye.
In the dark of night, I felt you silently shed tears of loss and regret.
All I could offer was comfort and love.
Your transition had begun!

In numbness, I couldn't wrap my mind around what was to come.
The finality of "it" ~ the loss of you ~ the loss of us loomed.
A wound was emerging that would seep into my heart
and into my being ... *it would change me forever!*

I am here alone now, looking at your picture, imagining
being in your arms; searching for signs of your presence.
Sadness permeates my heart, tears are wept, and I long for you.
Our love affair here on Earth has ended!

Life is a continuous spiral of events, which offers
each of us many welcomed and unwelcomed lessons.
With that in mind, I now understand that
my own transition has begun!

Laurel

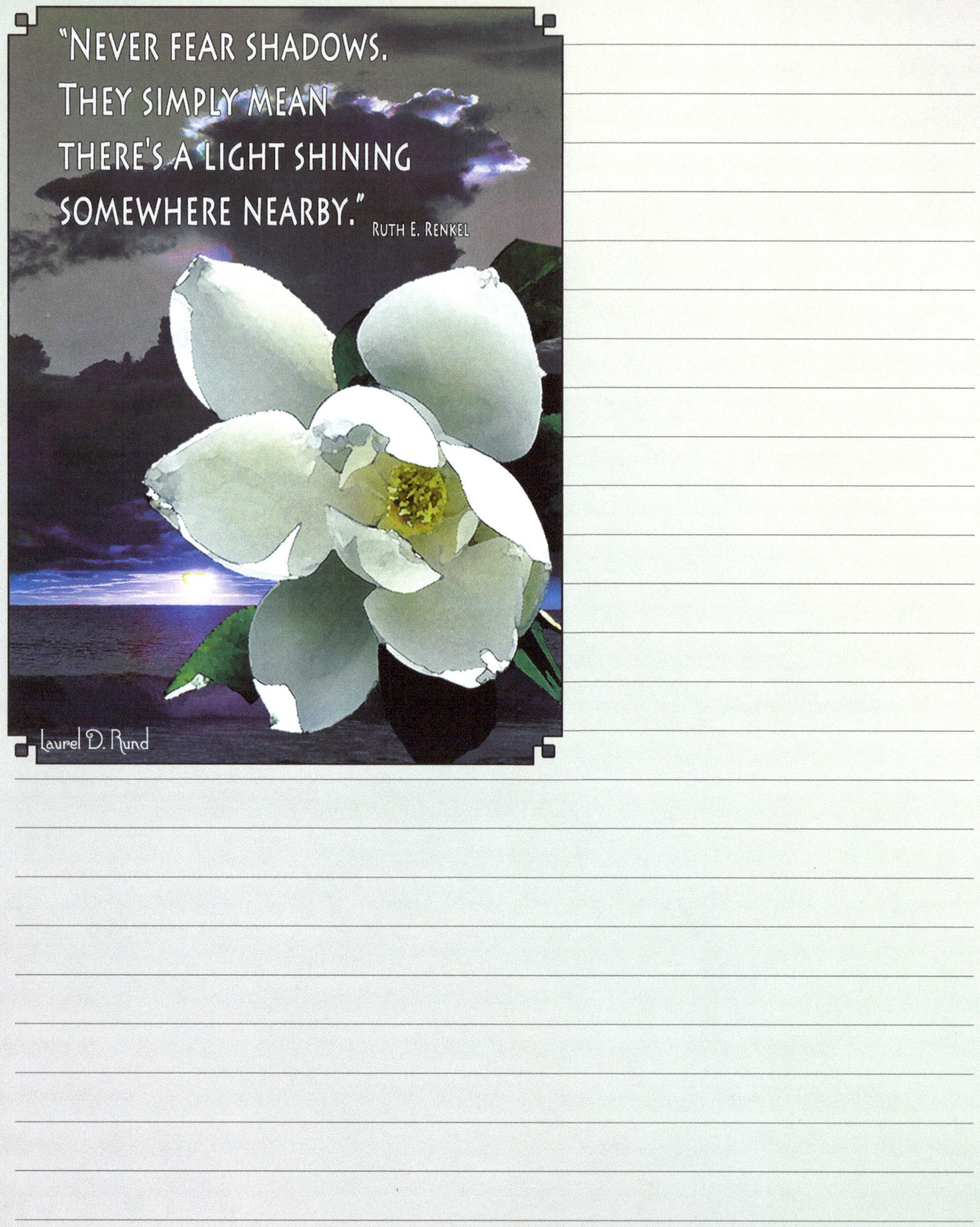
"NEVER FEAR SHADOWS.
THEY SIMPLY MEAN
THERE'S A LIGHT SHINING
SOMEWHERE NEARBY."
RUTH E. RENKEL
Laurel D. Rund

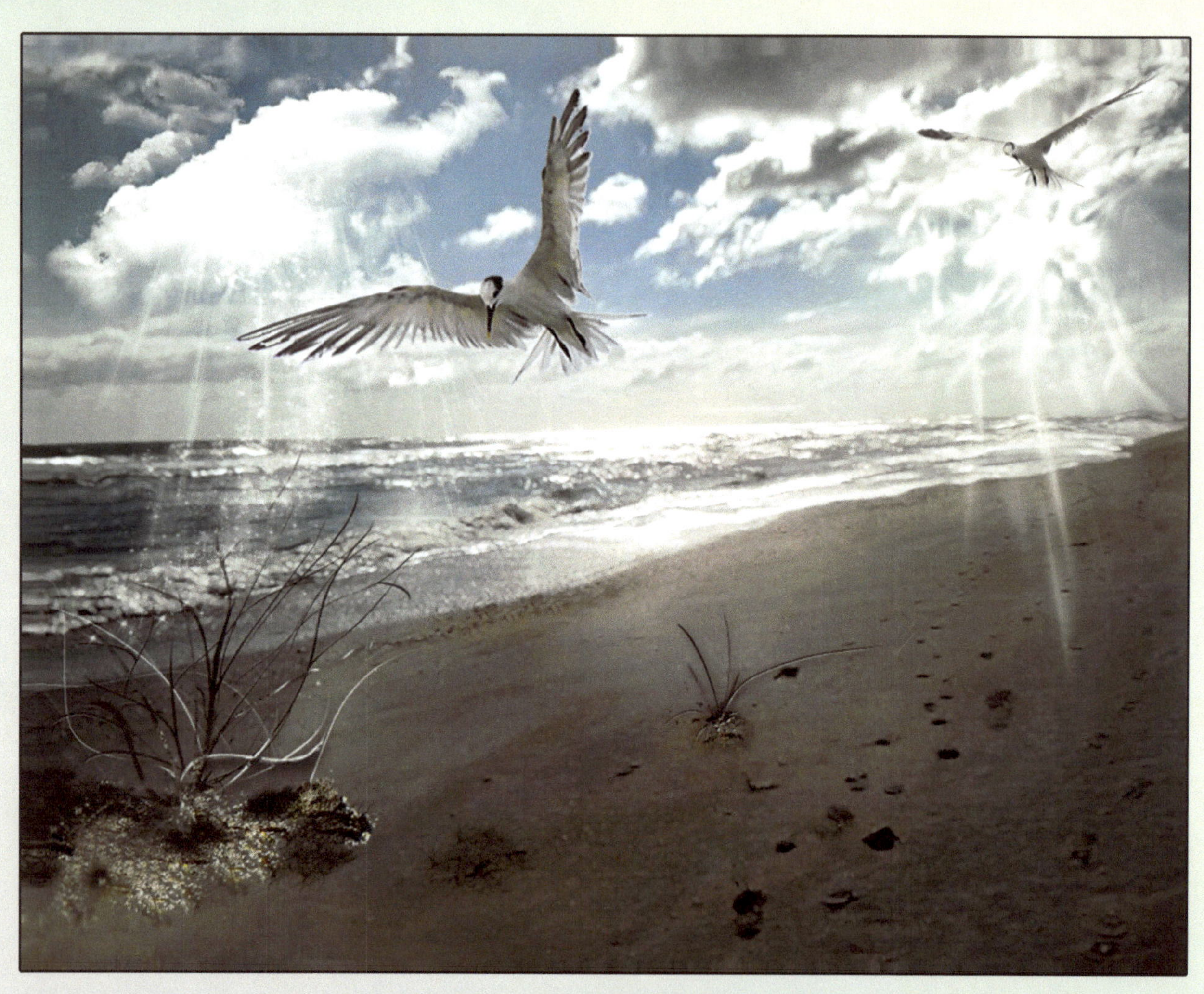

The Spirit of Flight

Grief's Undertow

Walking the beach, wading at the water's edge ~
stepping gingerly on shells broken by the force of nature.
I watch the sun cast its light over the ocean and wonder …

Where are you?
Can you see me?
Are you here?

Reflecting on these questions,
I am caught unaware.
A wave crashes in and knocks me off my feet,
dragging me into grief's undertow.
It is a deep, dark and turbulent place!

Tears pour out of me as I gasp for air ~
drowning in despair and sorrow.
Slowly, deliberately, the wave subsides and
pushes me back to the shore.
Unsteady, I regain my footing,
aware of the grief within my heart.

Remembering your final wishes for me,
and knowing that your spirit will always surround me,
I push myself forward to savor life ~
determined to live on!

Laurel

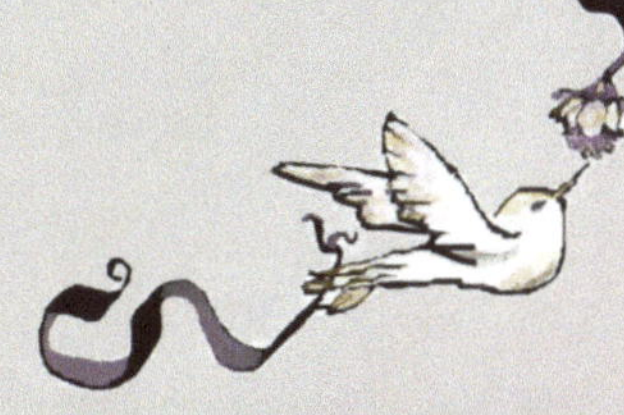

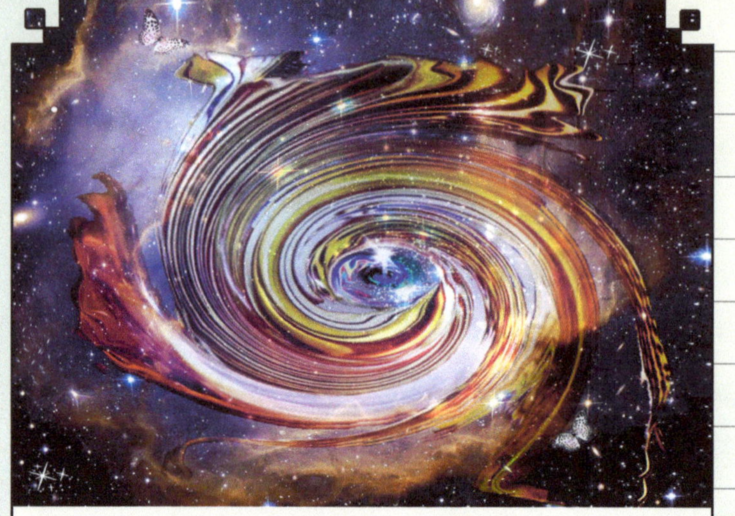

Eternity

Laurel D. Rund

WHAT THE CATERPILLAR CALLS

THE END OF THE WORLD,

THE MASTER CALLS A BUTTERFLY!

Richard Bach

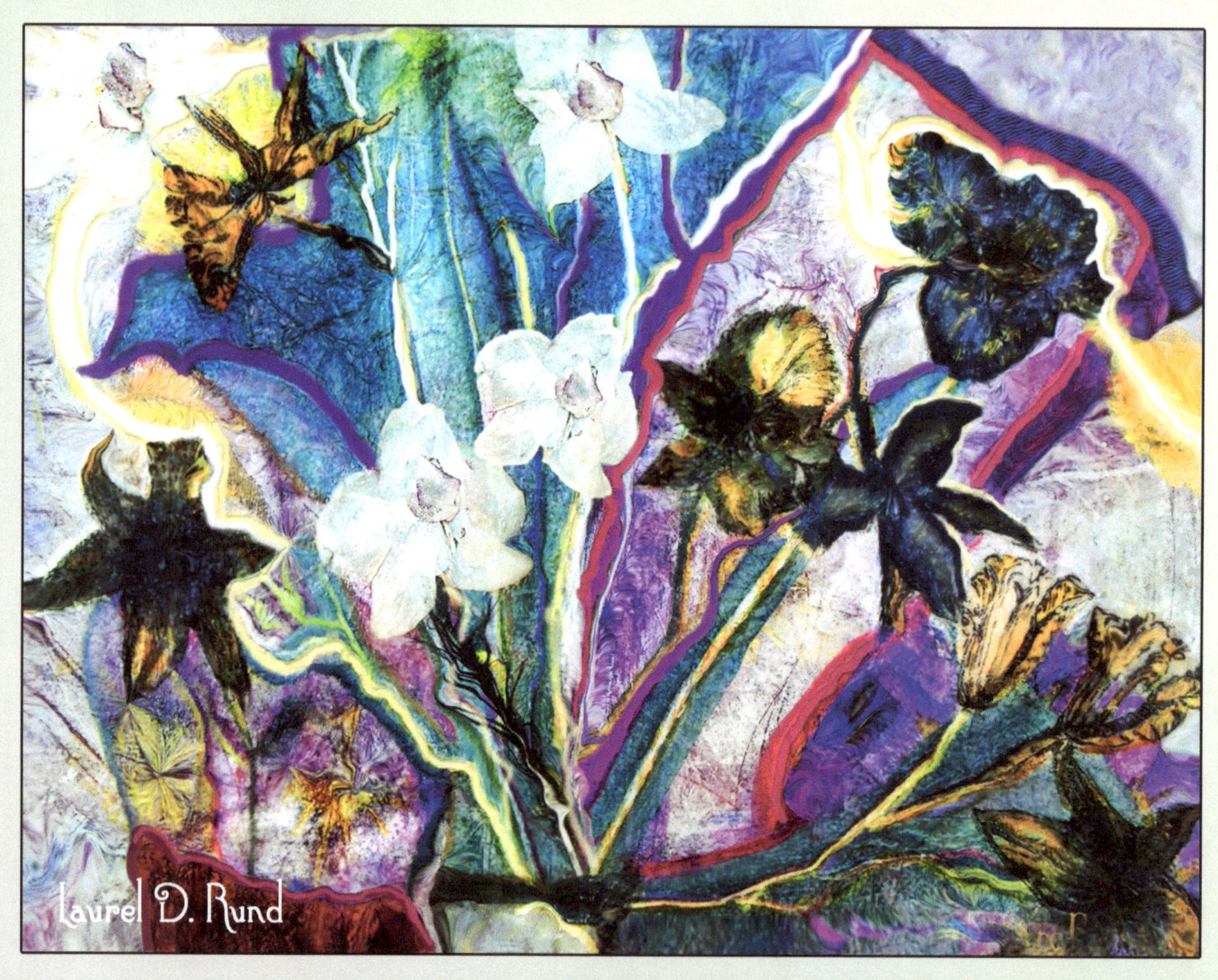

Emerging

Emerging Voices

There were so many voices in her head since his death, and they meshed into an angry crowd within her. These discordant sounds pulled her into an abyss called "grief." As the voices blended together, she could not hear them clearly, drown them out or turn them off. It was a time of profound sadness and she was uneasy, off balance ~ in a dark place that didn't seem to have an "*Exit*" sign within sight.

At other times, the voice of grief came in at a different frequency ~ like a low, annoying and distracting hum, with no shut-off valve to be found. It left her feeling agitated, disoriented and unsure as how to move forward … how to put one foot in front of another. It seemed as if daylight had arrived and was out of reach ~ too far in the distance for her to see.

Then, with the passing of time, a soft voice began to emerge from within. Eerily quiet and without static; it was gentle, compassionate and encouraging. Perhaps it was guided by powers beyond her understanding or her grasp, but it didn't really matter because she knew instinctively that she was hearing her own voice, her own spirit. So, she turned inward and listened. To her surprise, as the fog of sorrow lifted, she experienced visions of clarity, glimmers of hope and tiny moments of happiness.

It was then that she understood the voice of grief had been comforted ~ not put away ~ but eased. She had finally found the "*Entrance*" sign to her new life and intuitively knew that she was *Emerging*!

Laurel

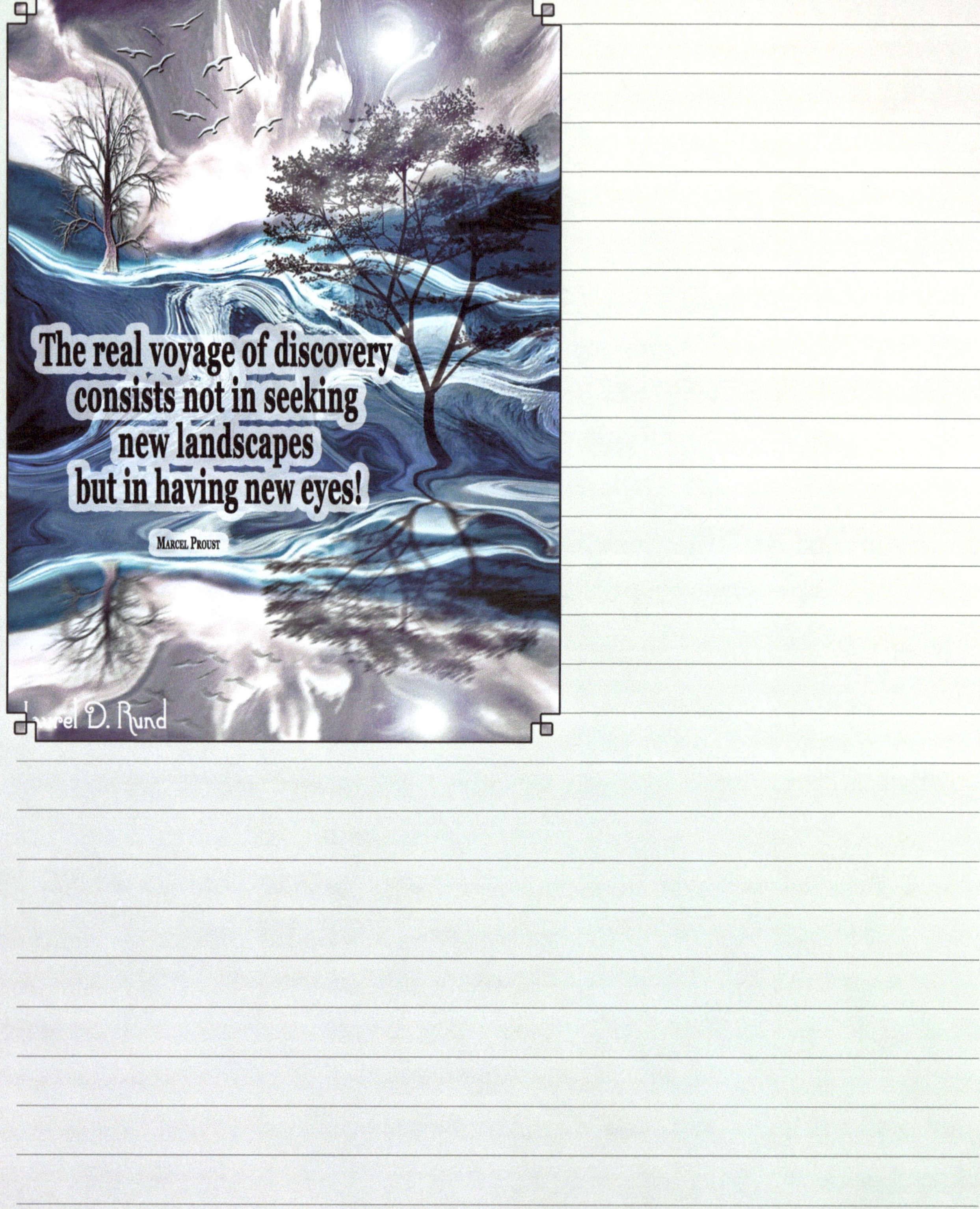
The real voyage of discovery
consists not in seeking
new landscapes
but in having new eyes!
Marcel Proust
Laurel D. Rund

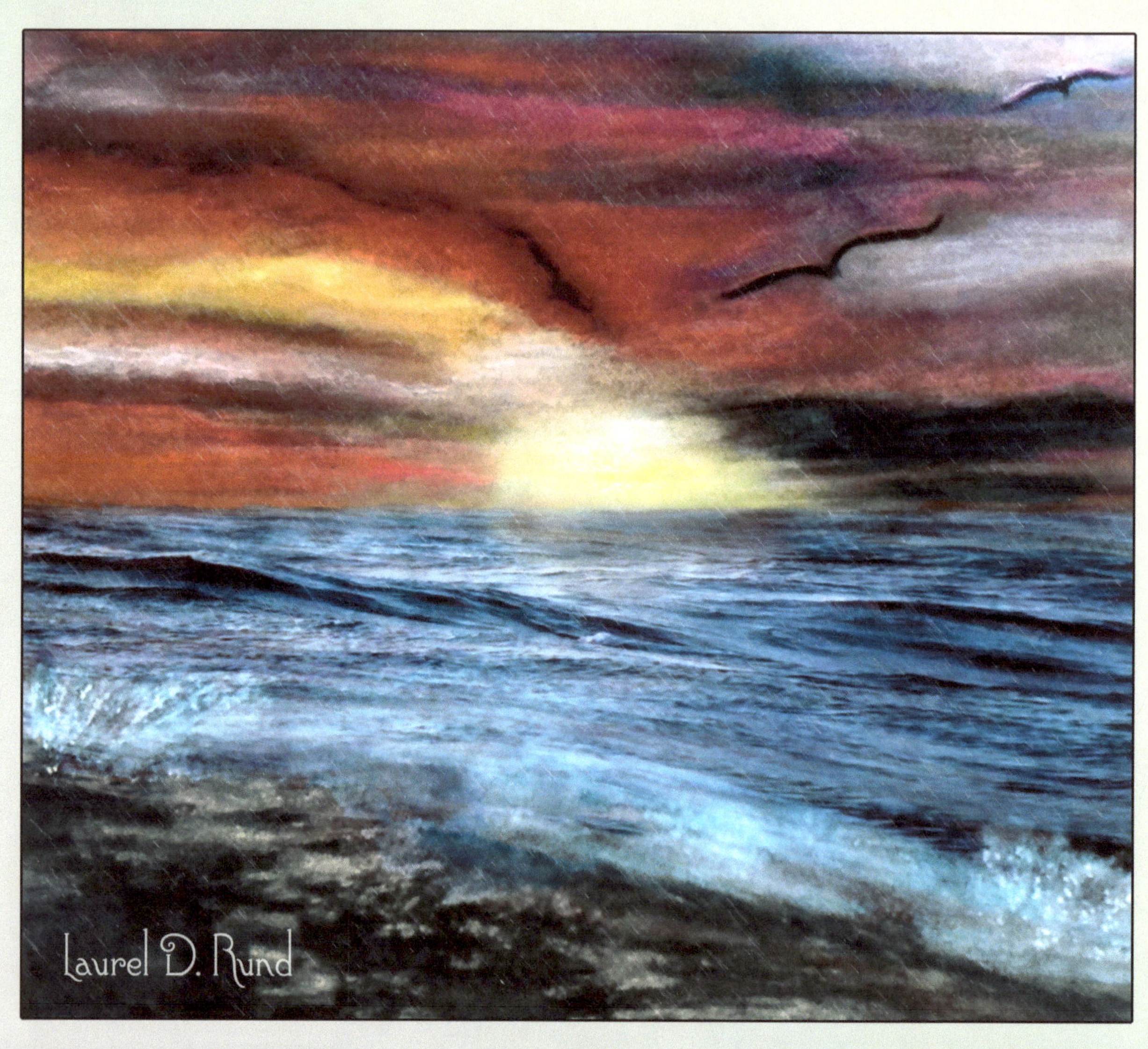

After the Storm

Grief's Cloak

I took off grief's cloak so that its heaviness would be removed.
I needed to lift this shroud of pain and sadness
in order to find out where and who I was without you.

Little by little, the light within me was rekindled.
With a newfound sense of freedom, I grew wings,
felt myself flying, raised up ~ joyous!
Grief's cloak vanished as I flew.

Riding the waves of life's currents, I found myself able to soar
without fear or sorrow coursing through my veins.
Experiencing things long postponed, rediscovering life's possibilities ~
my spirit overflowed with a rainbow of imaginings.

But wait! Was I also trying to outrun grief? No hide and seek here,
it was up ahead ~ my mourning was not complete.
Grief's cloak is a harsh reminder that loss is real ~
it cannot be pushed away!
And, if not accepted, even honored,
it will clip my wings and leave me unable to fly.
With this in mind, I have learned to say
"Welcome back Grief ~ I acknowledge your presence!"

In death there are no real endings.
The story of us is woven into the fabric of my wings,
and you are forever in my heart!
Remaining connected, even though we are in different forms and space.
You ahead of me, lighting the way ~ the wind upon which I soar,
the sunlit clouds upon which I perch.
Your spirit gently guides me and reminds me that
it is now time to chart my own course.

Laurel

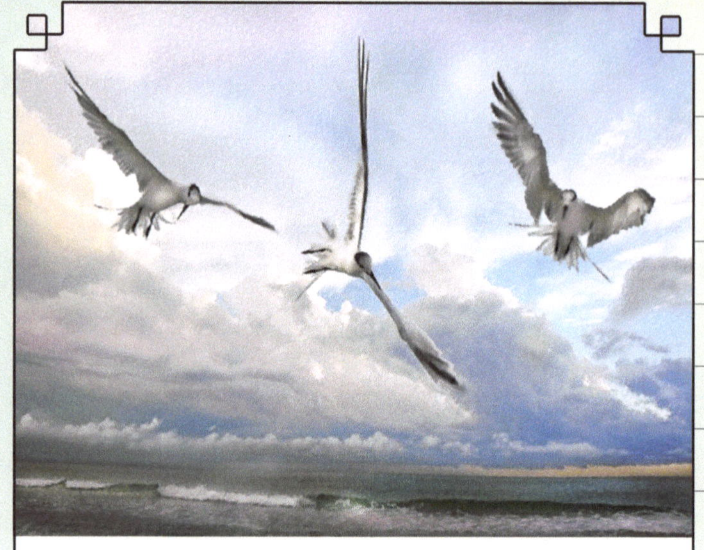

Freedom of Flight

Laurel D. Rund

Travelers, it is late.
Life's sun is going to set.
During these brief days that
you have strength,
be quick and spare no effort
of your wings.

Rumi

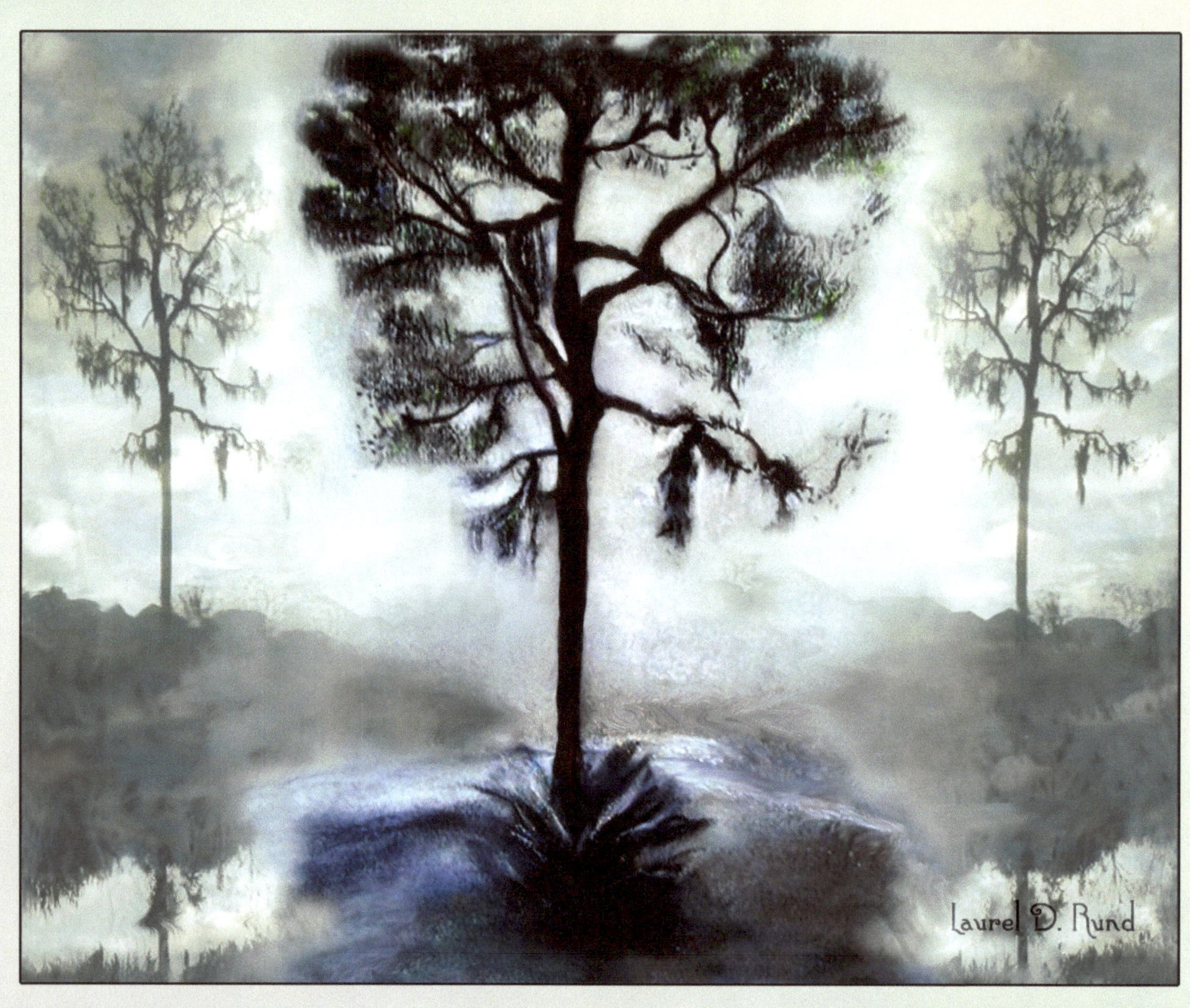

Elegy to a Tree

Elegy to a Tree

Welcoming all to a vision of grandeur, you stood tall and proud
with your trunk rooted firmly into the ground.
As your limbs reached towards the heavens,
I watched in awe as playful birds rested on your bare branches
and marveled when your sparse limbs were
illuminated by gleaming sunbeams.

You withstood the force of fierce winds, unrestrained rainstorms
and seemed to revel as lightning danced raggedly around you.
During your time on Earth, your spirit was one of
beauty, dignity, grace and, above all, courage.

Then, suddenly one day you disappeared!
Thoughtlessly cut down to fulfill man's need for youthful perfection,
you were replaced with a rather unremarkable seedling.
Was it time for your journey to come to an end
so that a new life could begin?
A reminder of one's mortality ~ your loss was jarring!

Know this "grand" tree ~
the image of your magnificent strength and glory
will always hold an honored place in my heart.

Laurel

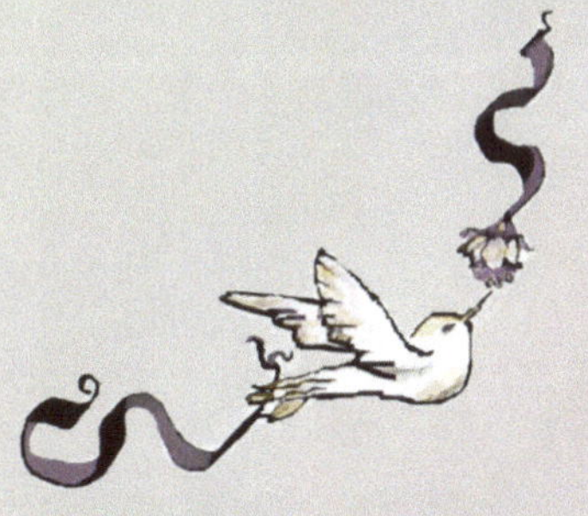

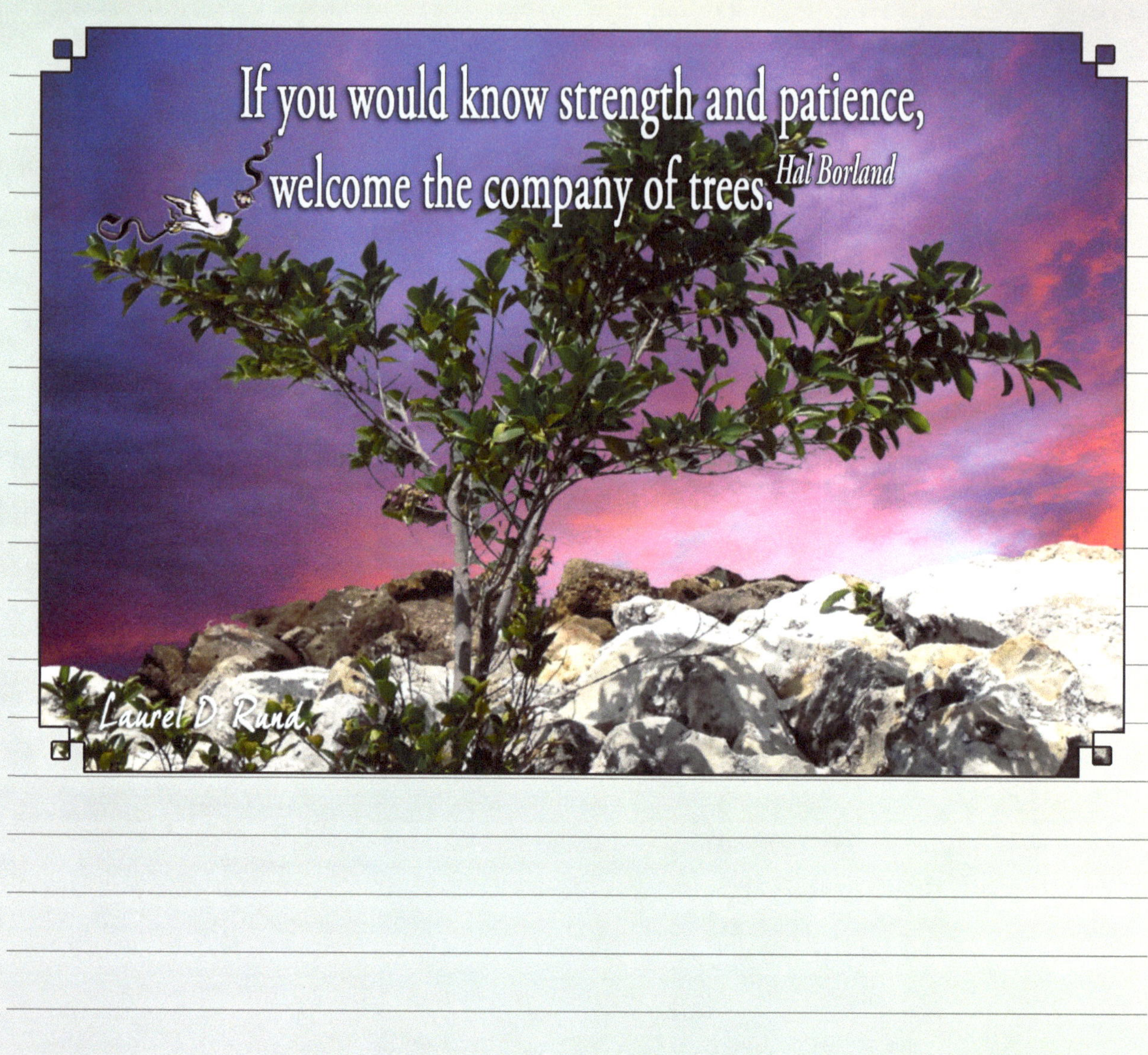
If you would know strength and patience,
welcome the company of trees.
Hal Borland
Laurel D. Rund

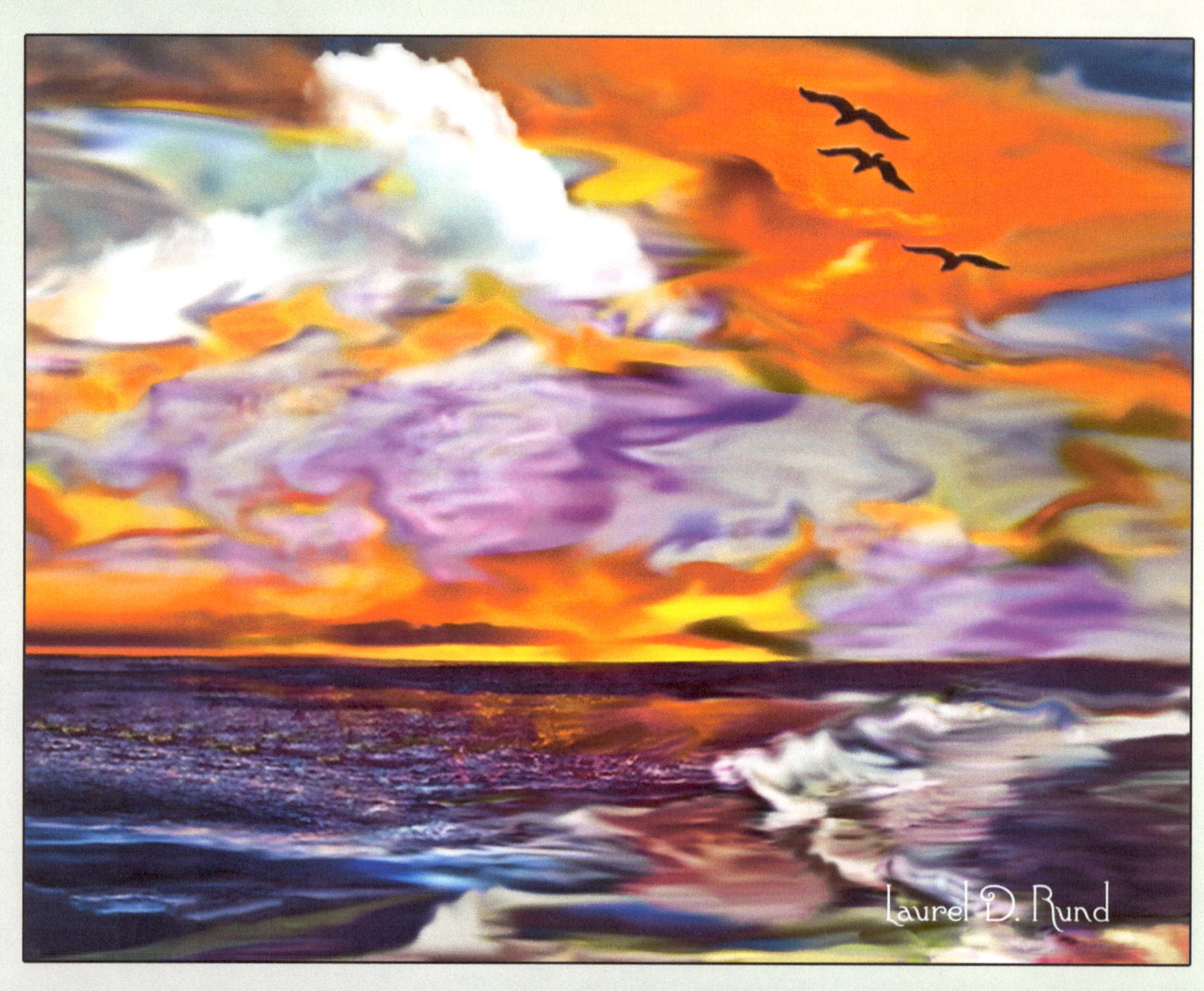

Endings and Beginnings

Endings and Beginnings

When I gaze at a sunset, it fills me with awe.
Watching the orange glow of the sun recede,
it takes me to a place of serenity and optimism.

As sundown arrives, I cannot help but
stand still … be quiet … and bear witness.
Nature's golden moments and breathtaking beauty
offer the gift of tranquility.

A sunset brings with it the soft whisper
of life's possibilities ~
the promise of a new day!

When this magnificent source of light
recedes behind the clouds far into the horizon,
and daylight starts to dim,
I know with certainty that life
always renews itself with
Endings and Beginnings.

Laurel

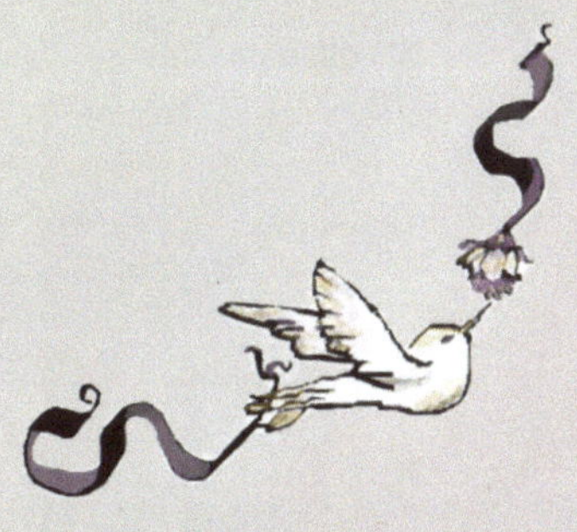

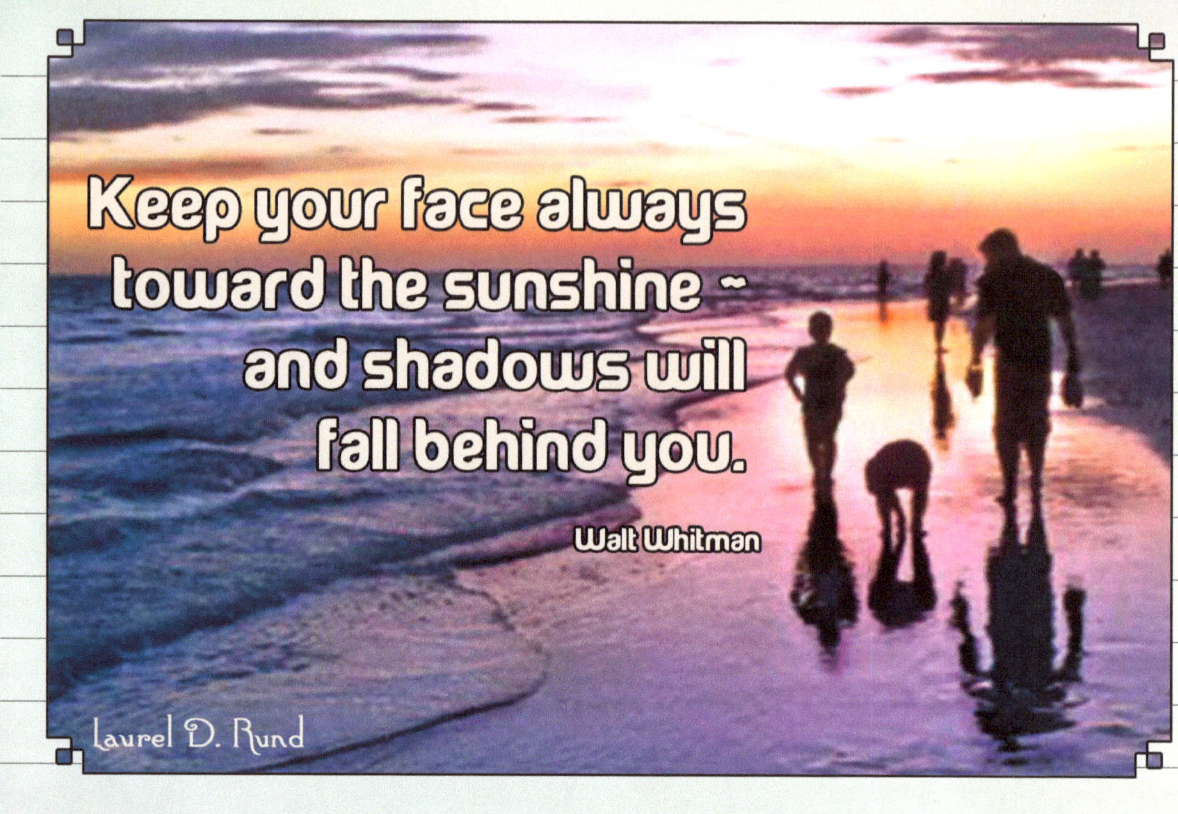
Keep your face always toward the sunshine ~ and shadows will fall behind you.
Walt Whitman
Laurel D. Rund

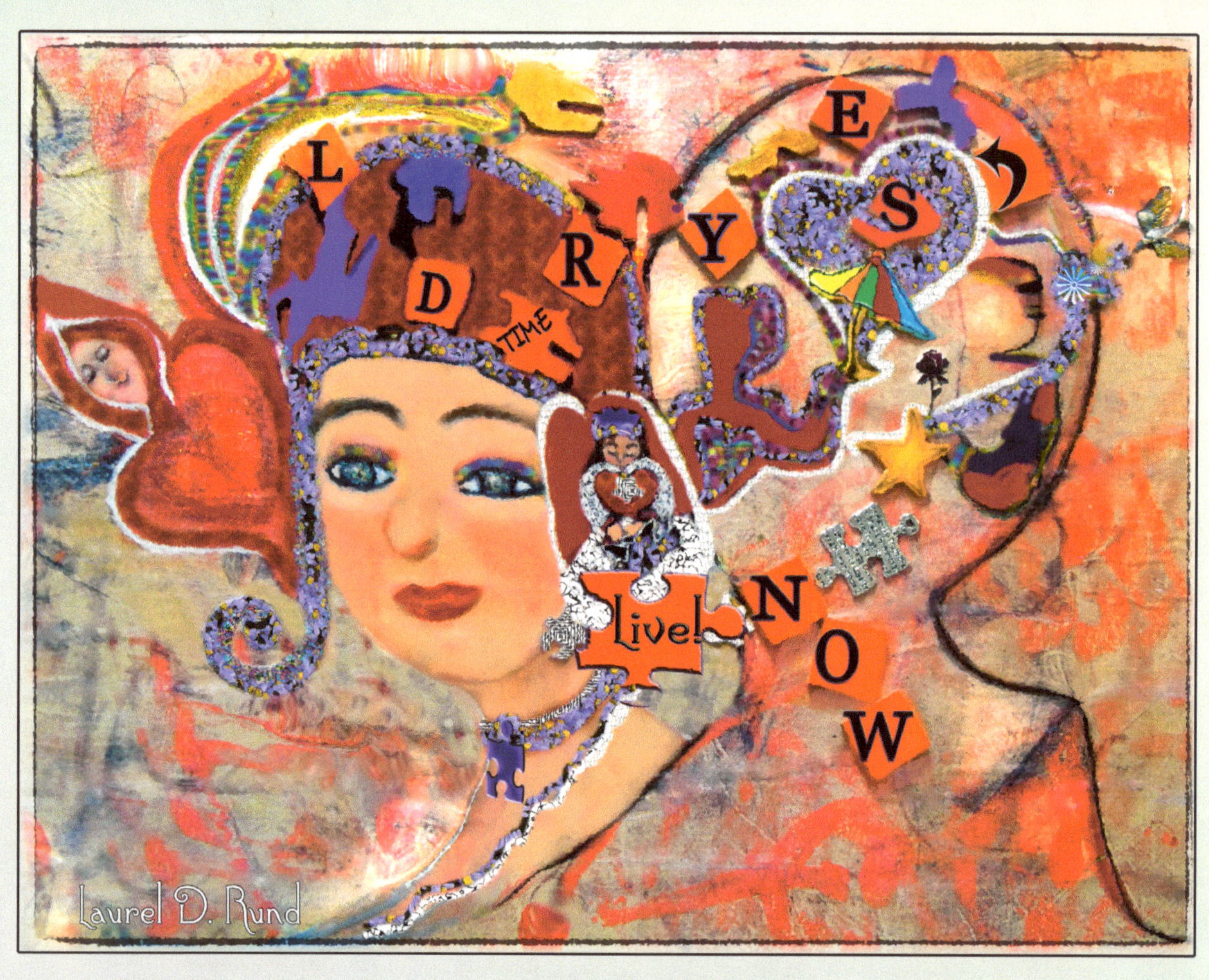

This Puzzle Called Life

This Puzzle Called Life

Pieced together throughout the years,
the outside border of this puzzle called "life"
presents itself as my human form.
Like a comfy pair of shoes, it is easy to wear
and visible for all to see.

Ah, but the inside pieces are much more
complex ~ hidden from view.
They are a reflection of my spirit, of my soul!
I have finally come to understand that these
puzzle pieces ought not be rigid or unyielding.
They should be sturdy, pliable and unrestrained
because life is about change and wisdom gained.

In the past, I was intimidated by puzzles,
put off by the frustration of not being able
to *see* how everything fits together.
Today, as I move my life's puzzle pieces around
and new shapes take form, I am filled
with curiosity and confidence.
These colorful images are a kaleidoscope which
reveal my intent, my purpose and the gifts within me.

Laurel

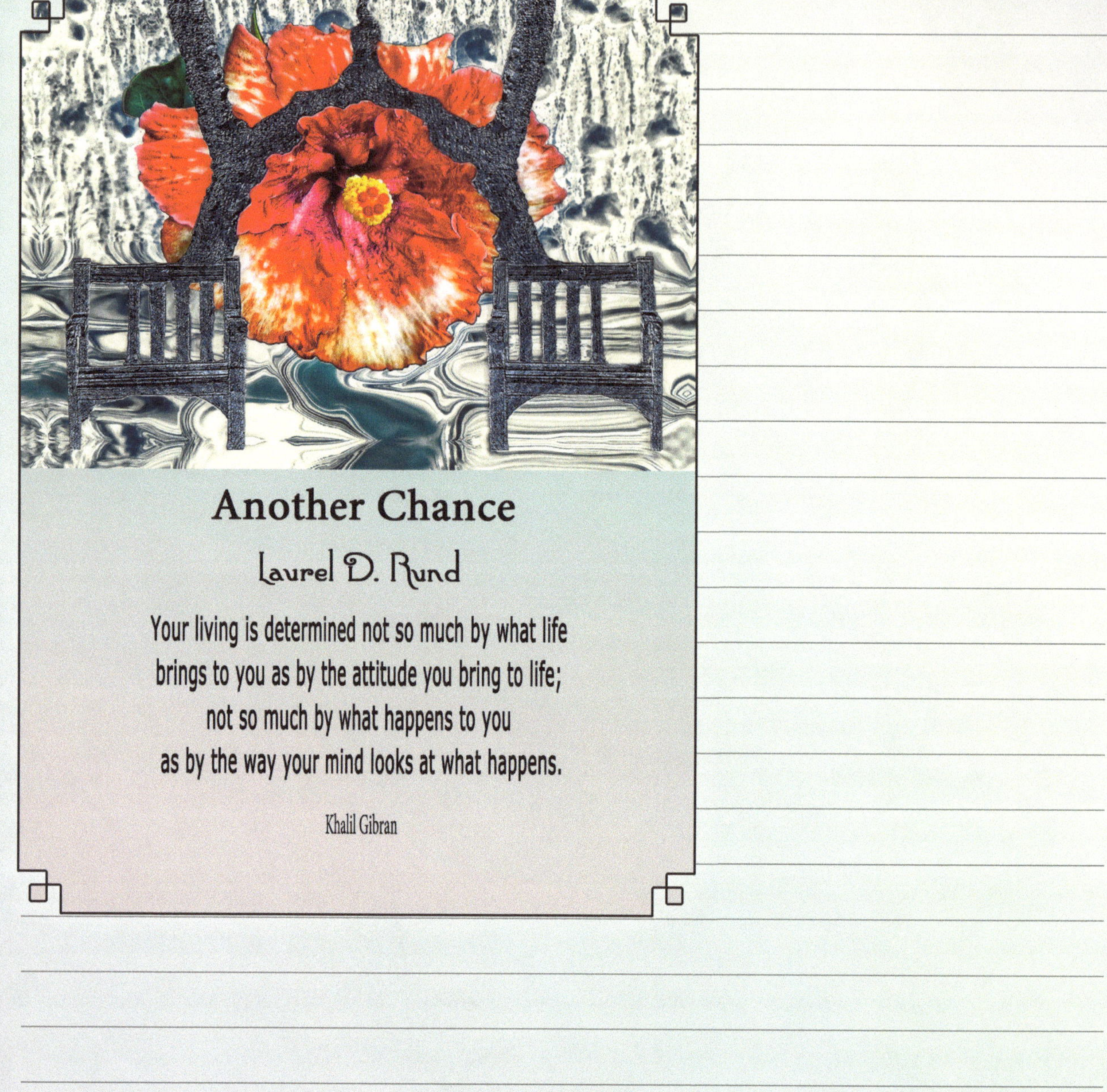

Another Chance

Laurel D. Rund

Your living is determined not so much by what life
brings to you as by the attitude you bring to life;
not so much by what happens to you
as by the way your mind looks at what happens.

Khalil Gibran

Solitary Firsts

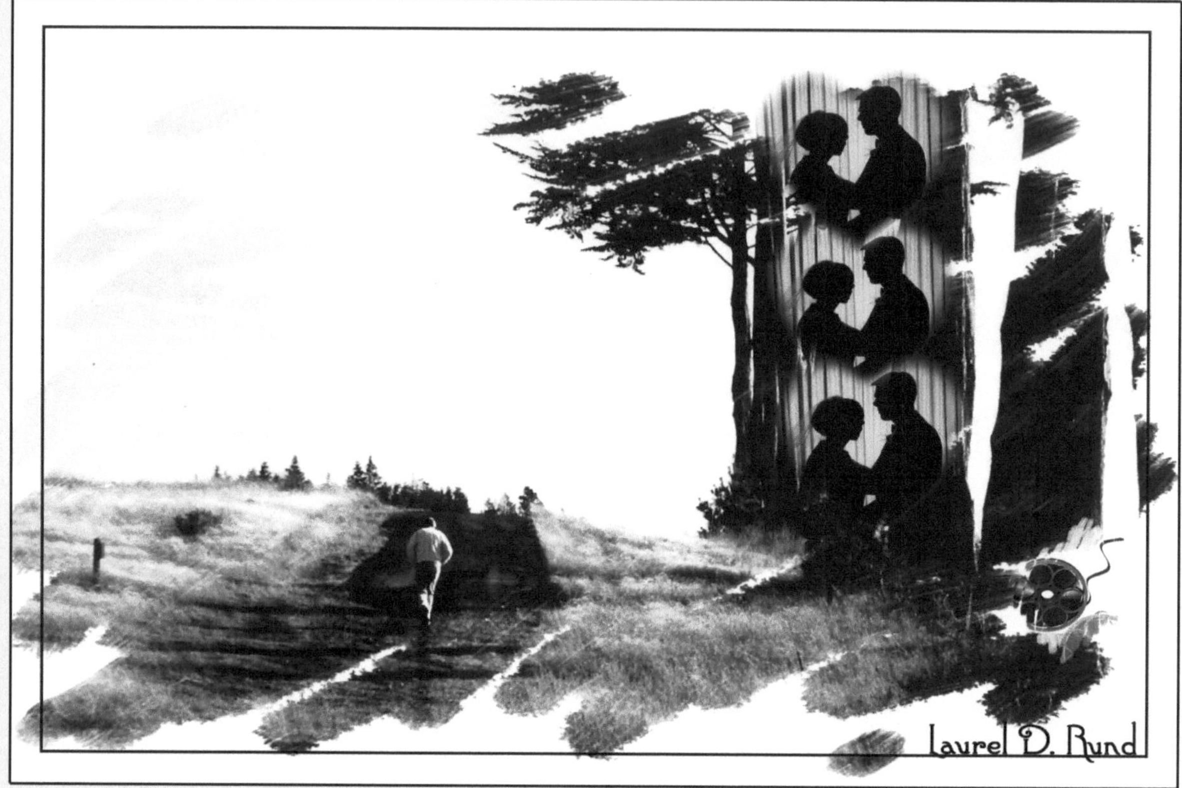

As I write this article, two years after my husband Marty's death, I am overwhelmed with surprise that so much time has passed and my memories are wrapped in a surreal haze. But, when vivid images surface and the fog lifts, I can still see and feel what happened during what I call "the year of *Solitary Firsts*."

*I*t began on February 11th, 2009 ~ the day of Marty's passing ~ three days before Valentines Day and eight days before our 42nd anniversary. Several days later, I flew to New York to attend Marty's *Celebration of Life*. I remember walking through the airport like a zombie, filled with angst and turmoil, wanting to scream out to anyone passing by, **"You don't understand … I just lost my husband!"**

While pressed up against the airplane window, trying hard to be invisible, I wrote to Marty. As tears rolled down my cheeks, I told him how alone I was feeling and about how hard it was for me to comprehend that I was going to his memorial service. A middle-aged couple sat down next to me and I yearned to say to them, "**your time together is precious and limited, don't take it for granted, don't waste it!**"

After the Celebration of Life service was over, I turned around to look for my husband to say, "*okay Babe, let's go home.*" Startled, ***my heart sank*** ... I had forgotten for a moment that he was *gone*. It was a harsh reminder that my Marty would never be there to go home to or be with again.

I don't remember the trip back to Florida. What I recall is the strong feeling that I just wanted to go home. When I returned and entered our house *to no one's arms*, or a "*hi Babe,*" it was surreal and grim. Yet somehow I felt comforted because it was the nest we had built together ~ and *Marty's energy was still palpable.*

There was a sense of his presence, and his absence, everywhere I turned. Marty's side of the bed was empty, his place at the kitchen table was bare, and his closet was filled with clothing that he would never wear again. I wandered around like a ghost and then wearily fell into bed, closing my eyes to the emptiness and my ears to the sounds of silence.

When I reached over in my sleep to touch Marty with my hand or foot, I would wake up with a start realizing that he wasn't there. Many times it would happen at 3 am. In a state of disbelief, I would say to myself, "*This was the time it happened; this was the time he died.*" For many months, sleeping and eating became an unwelcomed burden ~ what I had to do in order to survive.

I didn't have a big support system in Florida and recognized that I needed help coping with the pain of loss and grief. I pushed myself to meet with a hospice counselor who encouraged me to join a bereavement group. My healing began in this "safe" place ~ I was able to talk to hospice counselors who understood the grieving process and with group members who had also experienced loss. It was okay to not be *"all right"* in the bereavement group. That was where I learned there are no "rules" for how to grieve or how long it "should take."

*S*ometimes I liken that first year to a soldier returning from war with post-traumatic stress disorder. Images would flash before my eyes at unexpected moments. When I passed a building associated with Marty's illness, I would shudder; when I saw an emaciated person who looked ill, I would lose my breath and look away.

*R*ituals started to emerge. I wrapped myself in Marty's bathrobe and sprayed it with his cologne at night ~ envisioning his arms wrapped protectively around me. During that first year, I journaled letters to my husband, telling him how I was feeling or what was happening in my life. Every morning I would write him a love note on the steamy glass shower wall. I wore Marty's watch and his Chai necklace because it felt like his "*energy*" was with me. As a reminder, I calendared a note to myself (as if I would forget) to light a memorial candle on the 11th of each month ~ which I did for that entire year.

*W*hen it came time to pick up Marty's ashes, I felt anxious and filled with dread. Driving to the crematorium on my own, I was in a state of suspended disbelief over what I was doing. But, when the container holding his ashes (a beautiful wooden box, lovingly handmade by my brother) was placed in the car, a sense of calm came over me. *I felt like I was taking my husband home*. Even though I did not believe the ashes contained Marty's "spirit," I placed them on a credenza facing the golf course ... perchance there was a bit of his "energy" in there. I wanted him to be able to watch the sport he loved so dearly.

I called home many times to hear Marty's voice on the message machine. It took courage for me to change that recording, and I did so only when I was able to make a copy of his voice and store it safely on my computer. The new message said, *"I'm not home"* (not*"we're not home"*~ another powerful reminder that I was **alone**.)

*B*ecause the worst had already happened, I no longer had to live in a constant state of fear. Each day felt like a roller coaster ride, bringing with it something new and unanticipated. Sometimes I was filled with raw emotions and sadness ~ at other times it was a day which offered me slivers of hope and optimism.

I began enrolling in art and writing classes, forming new friendships, and living life as a single woman. It was a transformative time during which I began to experience a sense of renewal ... there were even days when I managed to smile and laugh once again!

To my chagrin, two months before the one-year marker, feelings of grief rolled back in and hit me hard. A torrent of fresh tears rained down, stirred by vivid memories and images of the times we fought to keep Marty alive. Despite the fact that the healing process had been softening my heartache, this felt like a huge setback.

As it got closer to the "Anniversary" *(why would anyone call the day someone dies an anniversary?)* I felt anxious and forlorn. The clock kept ticking as February 11th loomed. I just wanted "IT" ~ that day ~ to be over.

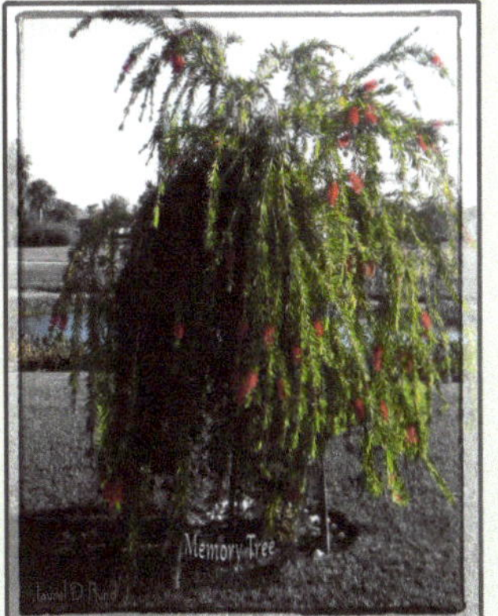

In the Jewish faith, it is tradition to put up a monument in a cemetery at the one-year anniversary. Instead, I decided to plant a ***living memorial*** to Marty ~ a Memory Tree. To honor his legacy, letters from my sons and their wives, my grandchildren and me, along with cherished pictures and mementos, were buried in the soil underneath its roots. The tree was planted in front of my office window so that I could watch it grow and become a landing place for butterflies and birds.

On February 11th, a few dear friends came and we held a dedication ceremony over my *Tree of Love*. It was at that time that I set an intention that the day of my husband's death would no longer be about loss. Going forward, it would be time to celebrate our shared life journey and to honor ***two transitions*** ~ both Marty's and mine.

A quote on the back of Joyce Carol Oates' book, *A Widow's Story,* says "of the widow's countless death-duties, there is really just one that matters: on the first anniversary of her husband's death, the widow should think 'I kept myself alive.' " When I read those profound words, I remember thinking, **"I did that!"**

Sometimes in the rush of life there are many symbolic moments which slip by without notice. After someone you love dies, the first year is filled with memories which are too countless to describe.

That year, my year of *Solitary Firsts,* is stitched into my heart and will be with me **for however long my forever is.**

Laurel

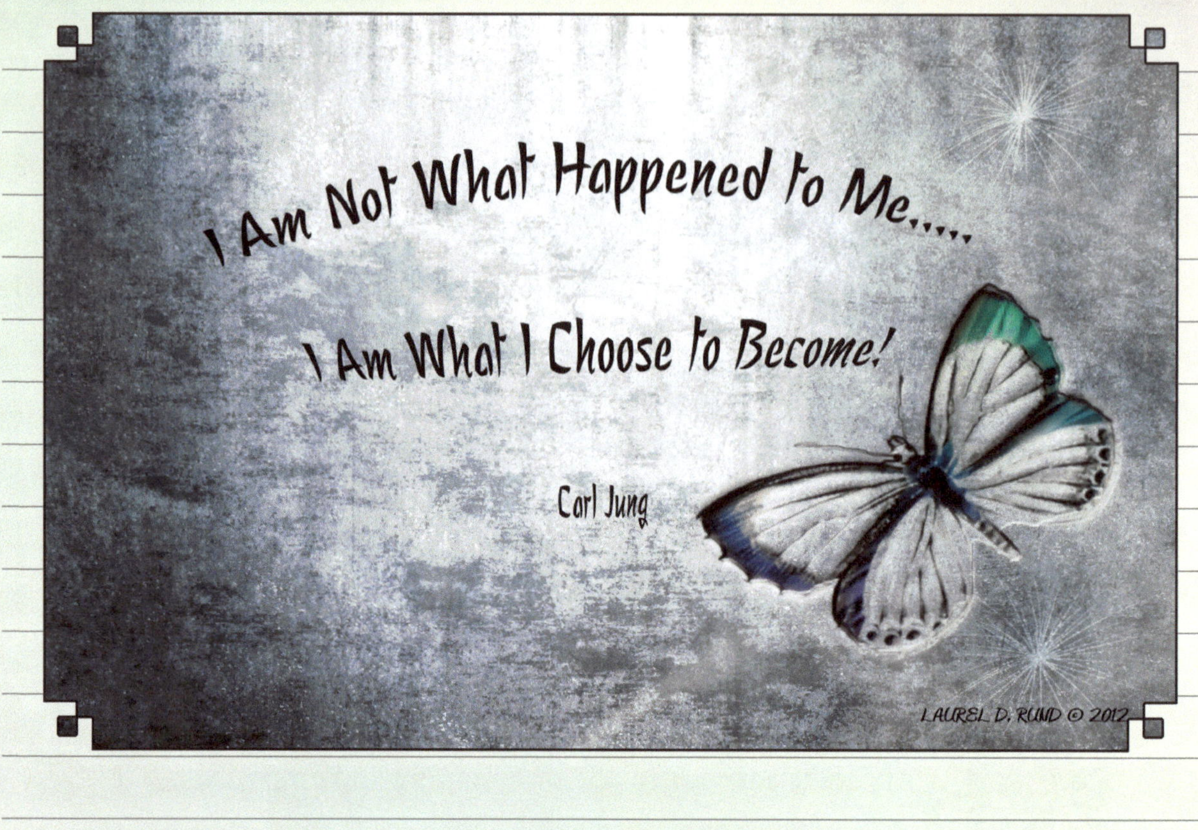
I Am Not What Happened to Me.....
I Am What I Choose to Become!
Carl Jung
LAUREL D. RUND © 2012

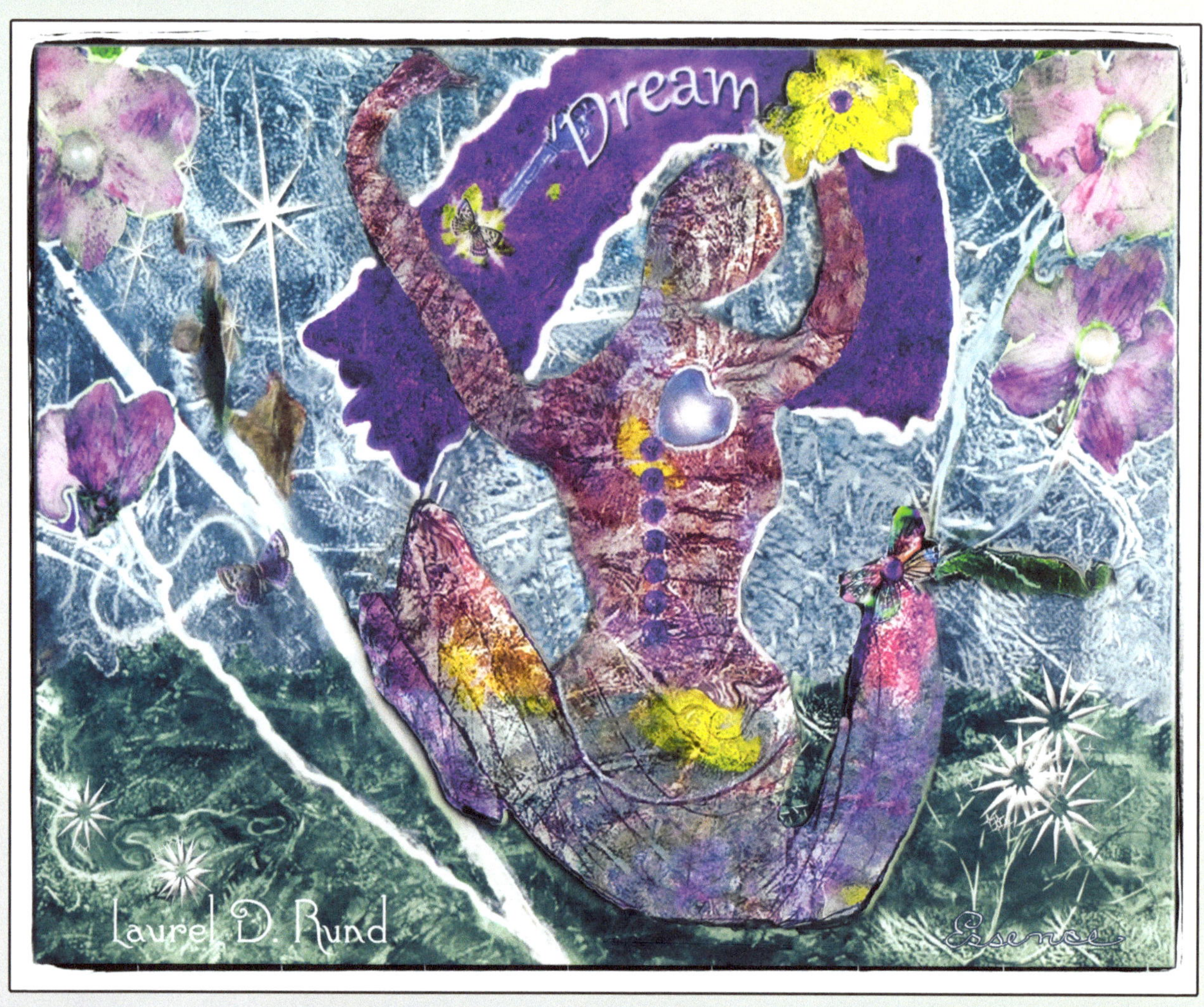

Essence

Essence

Can you see it?
Can you feel it?
Can you hear it?

My Essence has come alive once again!
It is remembering who I am,
who I was meant to be.

I have a newfound purpose,
a delight in spirit
and a joy-filled sense of being.
As I respond to what sparkles within me,
my aura lightens and is warmed
by life's embrace.

Life's possibilities are the ingredients
which encourage me to blossom.

Can you see it?
Can you feel it?
Can you hear it?

My *Essence* is unfolding and
dancing to the rhythm of my heart.

Laurel

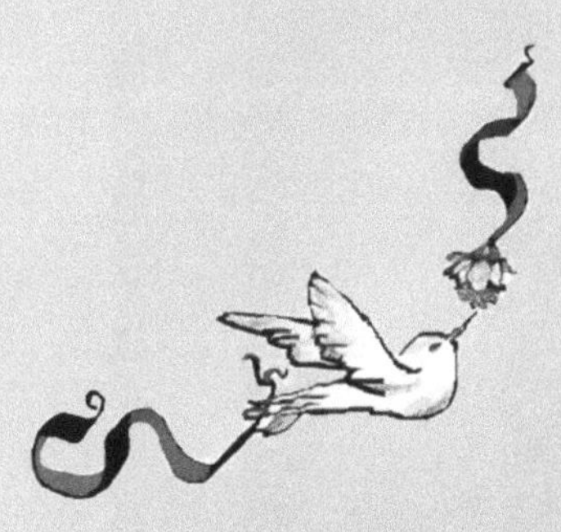

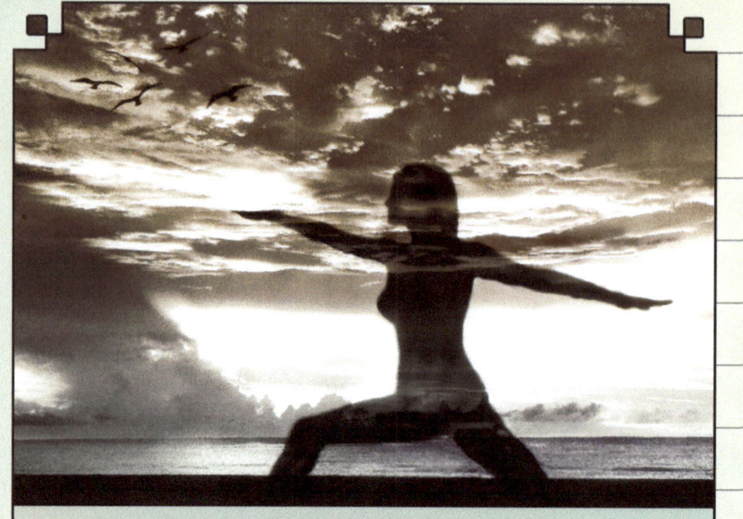

Reaching for Sunset

Laurel D. Rund

Clouds come floating into my life,
no longer to carry rain
or usher storms,
but to add color to my sunset sky.

Deepak Chopra

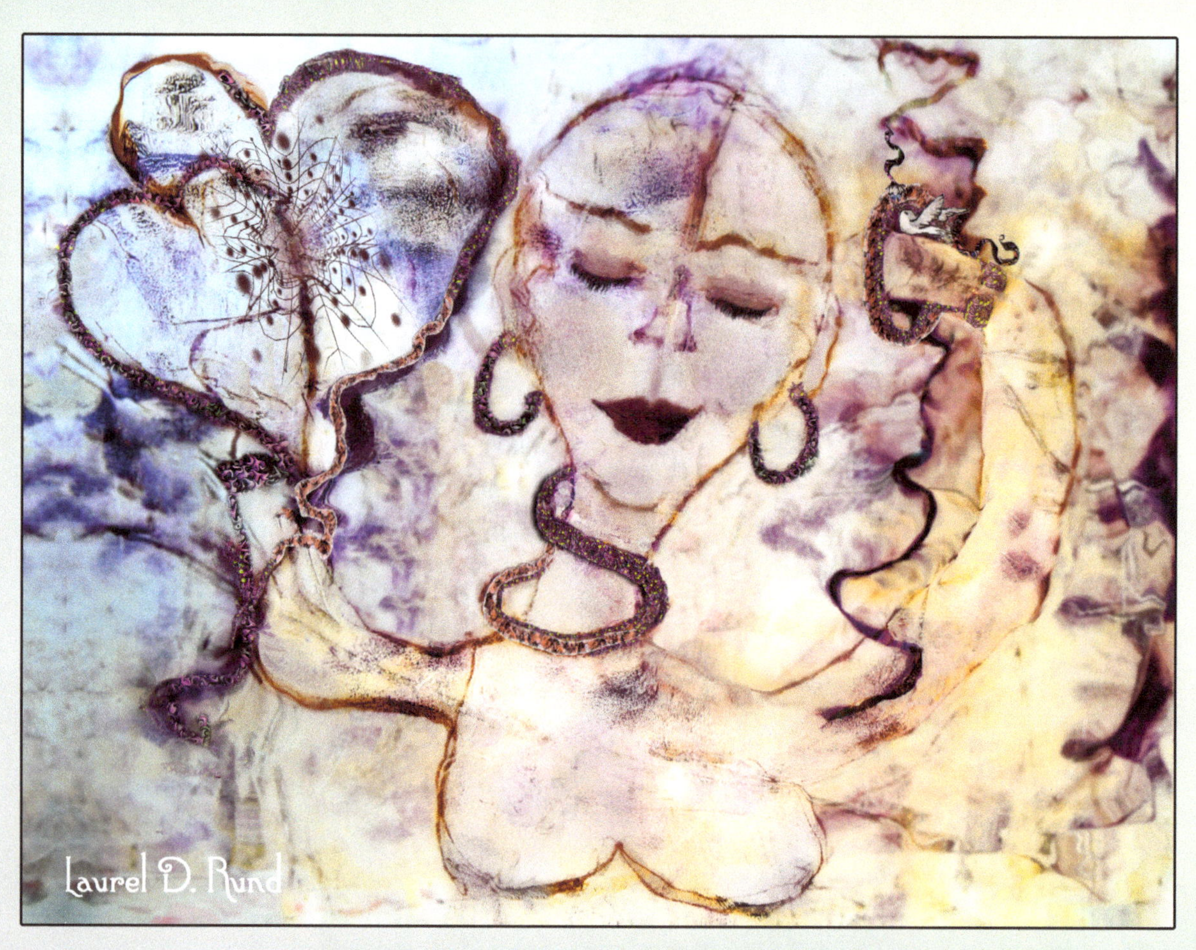

Body Language

Laurel's Kitchen

By chance, a friend happened upon
a cookbook named *"Laurel's Kitchen."*
The serendipity of this discovery
gave me pause to reflect about my life.

Just what are the ingredients that will create
a delectable and scrumptious dish?
In what exact order should the measurements be added?
How does everything get kneaded together?
Should I let the concoction sit undisturbed
until it all blends together and finds its balance?

How long will it take to cook up a *perfect* dish?
And, when tasting this mixture, will I remember to relish
what feeds my heart and enriches my soul?

Life does not come with a cookbook!
Each day brings with it the promise for hope and renewal.
It is when I choose this recipe for *living*
I know I am in *"Laurel's Kitchen."*

Laurel

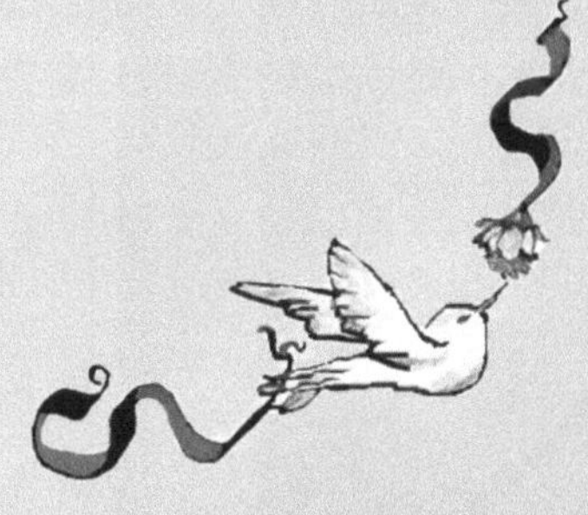

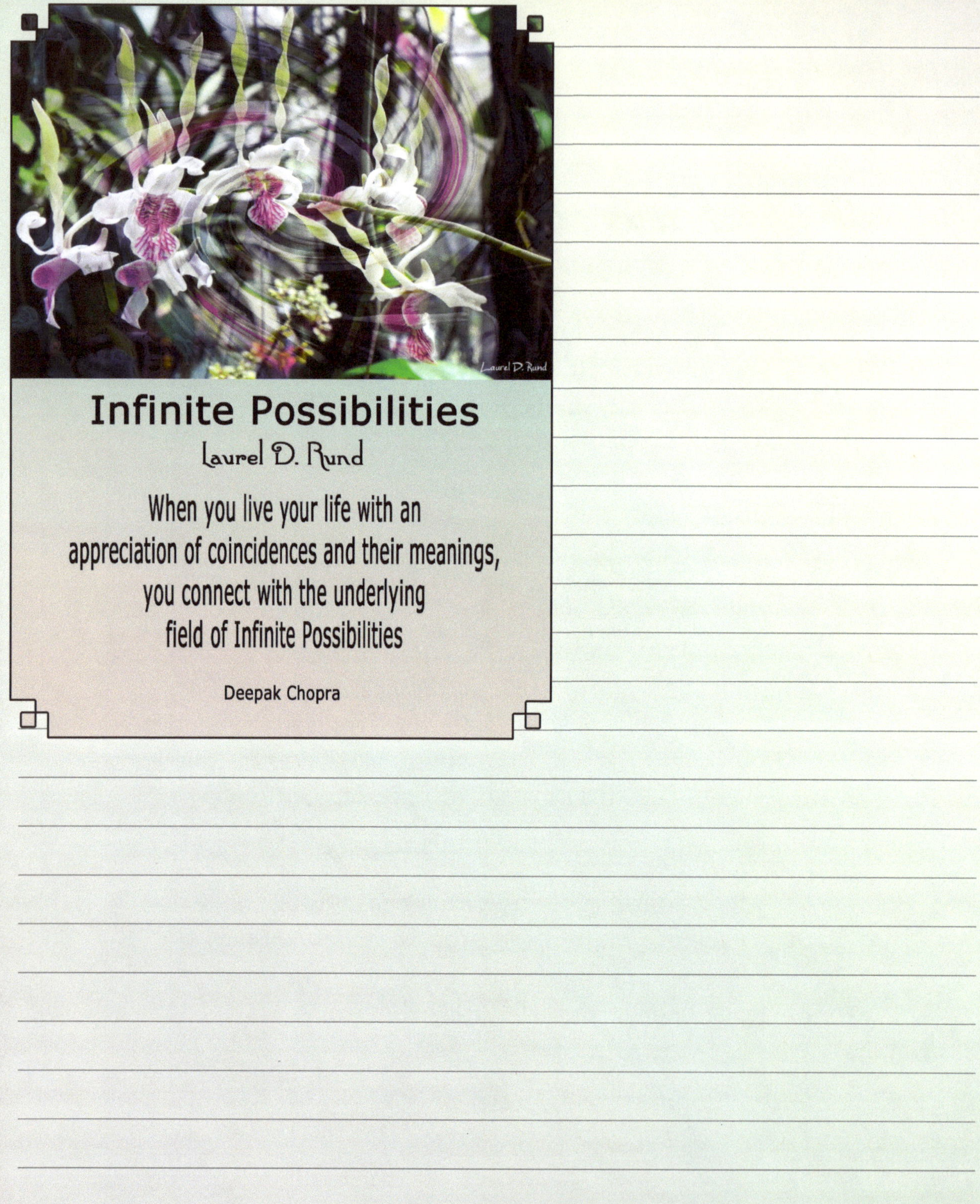

Infinite Possibilities

Laurel D. Rund

When you live your life with an
appreciation of coincidences and their meanings,
you connect with the underlying
field of Infinite Possibilities

Deepak Chopra

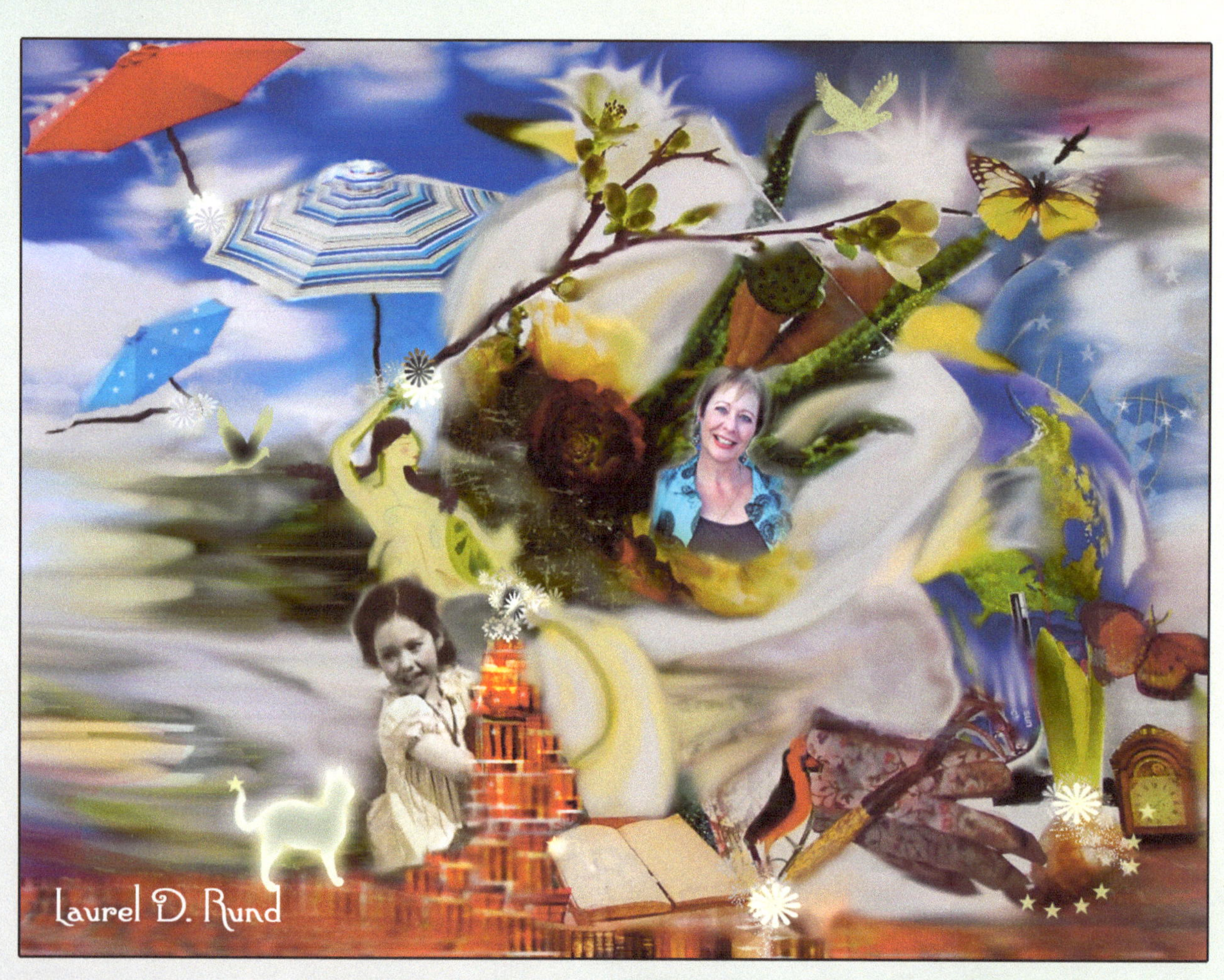

After All These Years

After All These Years

After all these years, I knocked at my inner child's door
and asked her to come out to play.
Although she was stored away and
hushed into silence for a very long time,
she appeared with an *infectious grin* on her face.

We decided to venture out, to live life fully ~
to blossom and become one!
When my inner child dances,
my feet move to a newfound rhythm.
When she steps on a crack,
I step outside my bounds.
When she giggles,
I laugh whole-heartedly and out loud.

When she loves, I am gentle and open.
And, when my inner child sings from her heart,
I sing from my soul!
As I hold her hand in mine,
the child within me has been transformed ~
and so have I!

Laurel

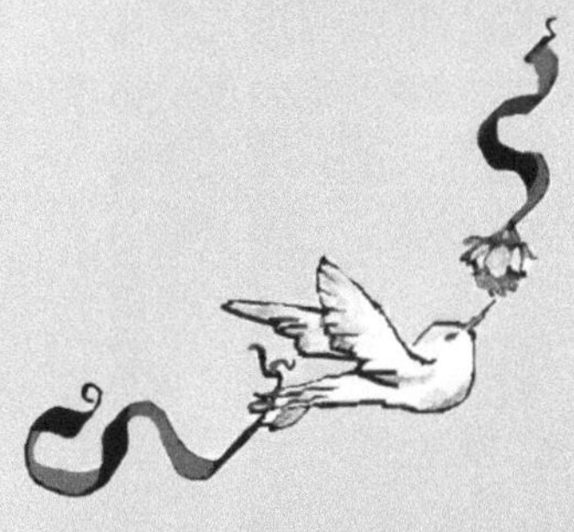

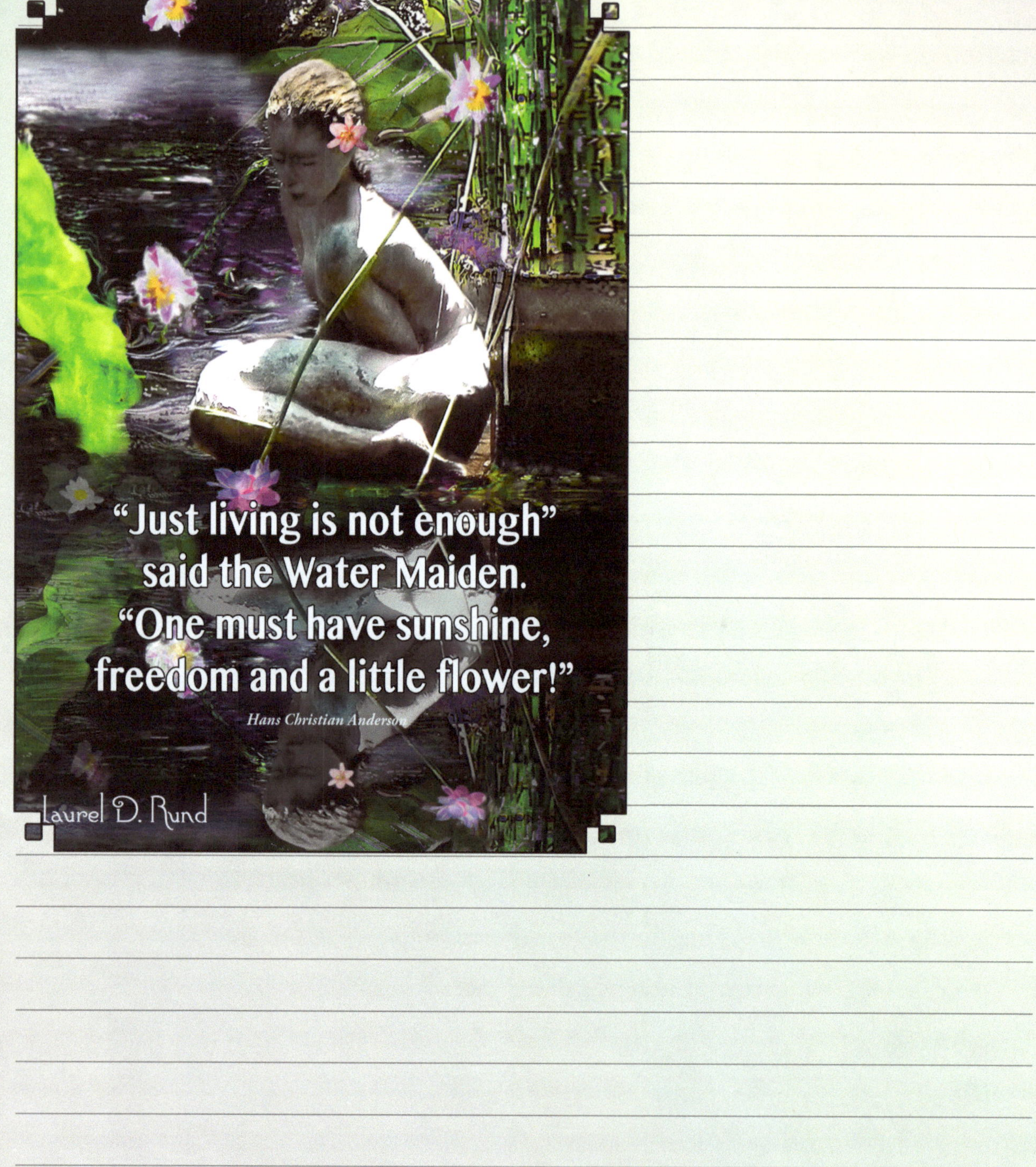
"Just living is not enough"
said the Water Maiden.
"One must have sunshine,
freedom and a little flower!"
Hans Christian Anderson
Laurel D. Rund

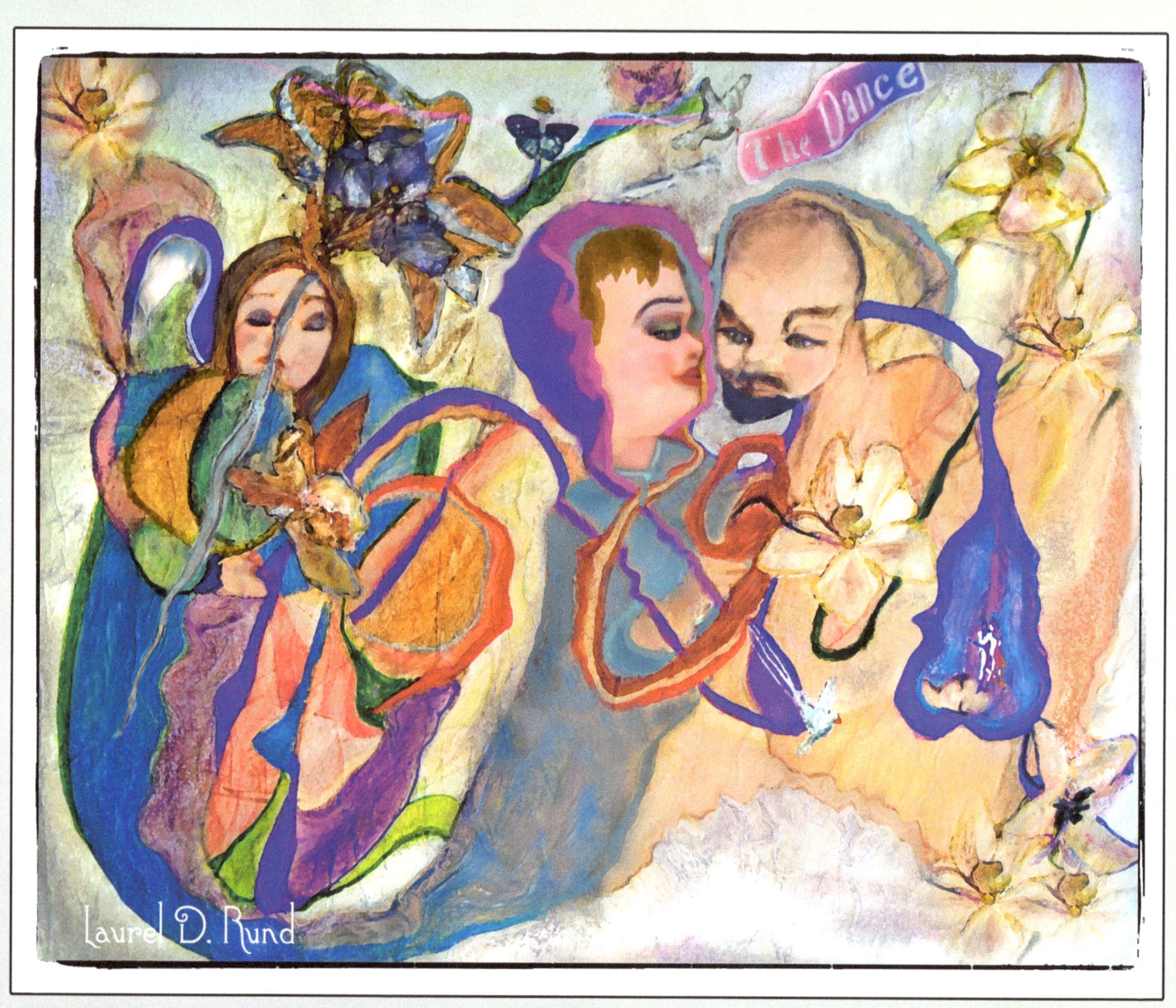

The Dance

The Dance

Sometimes someone dances into your life
and *twirls your heart around.*
Each step you take together lights up your world.
The rhythm is *captivating*, the music *inspiring.*
Your senses are heightened as you each lead and follow.
Everything looks brighter, tastes better ~
optimism is in the air!

And then, the music changes …
it is harsh and difficult to follow.
No matter how hard you try, you lose the beat.
Once again your senses are heightened ~
not to the dance, but to the *missteps.*

There is a push-pull which
throws you off track, throws you off balance.
Your instincts are whispering … *something is wrong.*
Nonetheless, you keep trying to get
back into step and on with the dance …
listening and waiting for that tantalizing rhythm
which made your heart race.

As the music fades off into the distance,
your hands *reluctantly let go.*
In that moment, your spirit is dimmed
and each dancer is left without a partner.

Once more you begin to search ~ seeking that special someone
who will unexpectedly dance into your life.
Hoping that you will find a partner who is
moved by the music of your soul and will
twirl your heart around !

Laurel

"We can't always choose
the music life plays for us
but we can choose
how to dance to it!"
Laurel D. Rund

JUST BE!

It's funny how you meet that special someone in your life at the most unexpected time. I was getting my hair done one day without any thought other than, *"I really, really need to have my roots colored"* ~ picture this, **a woman sitting in the beauty salon with her hair sticking up in tin foil wraps, looking as if she had stuck her finger in an electrical socket.** Now come on folks, this is supposed to be a place where you can look your worst so that you can look your best, *right*?

The woman who cuts and colors my hair, a friend of mine, was also working with a client sitting to the left of me (he was preoccupied with his iPhone.) I paid this man little attention. Why would I, this was my personal space to relax and be pampered. Out of the blue, my hairdresser decided to introduce me to this man. After squirming in protest (I was thinking ~ **how could you do this to me**!) I turned my head, put on a tepid smile and curtly said, "hello." I swiveled back in my chair to my "friend" and whispered to her, "**Are you crazy?**"

Well, the rest is history, as they say. The man and I began to talk. I must admit, his resonant voice attracted me. He said, "I like your name, 'Laurel' ~ what color flower is it?" Hmmm ... clever pick-up line if, I may say so. I nonchalantly replied, "If you really want to know who I am, just go to my website ... *EssenceofLaurel.com*." I thought that this would put an end to the conversation; but I also wanted him to know that the website personified who I was. Not to mention the fact that it included a picture of me **without my hair standing up at all angles**! *(Thank goodness I wasn't having my eyebrows colored, because then I would have looked like one of the Marx brothers.)*

It took a few seconds for this guy to go to my Essence of Laurel website (thank you iPhone.) After a few minutes he had a visible reaction ... my art and writing seemed to startle him in a good way. It was then that we actually began to have a real conversation. We could have been at a coffee shop or having a glass of wine together, the imagery of where we were faded away. It was what we were "*seeing*" in each other that piqued our mutual interest.

The long and the short of it is that we met for dinner, then a movie, and then on and on. However, my feelings started to unnerve me because I wasn't looking for a relationship with someone, and I wasn't detecting any red flags which told me to *"stay away."*

Having spent precious time getting back on my feet after the loss of my husband, and building a new life for myself, I didn't want to *lose my freedom.* It was a time of life-altering change and metamorphosis, and I was just getting used to a "**new normal.**"

*M*y creativity and spirituality were emerging bit by bit, and I was allowing joy, light and laughter back into my life. I didn't want anything or anyone to sidetrack me on my path of personal transformation ~ and was especially fearful about the "risk" of opening my heart to love once again.

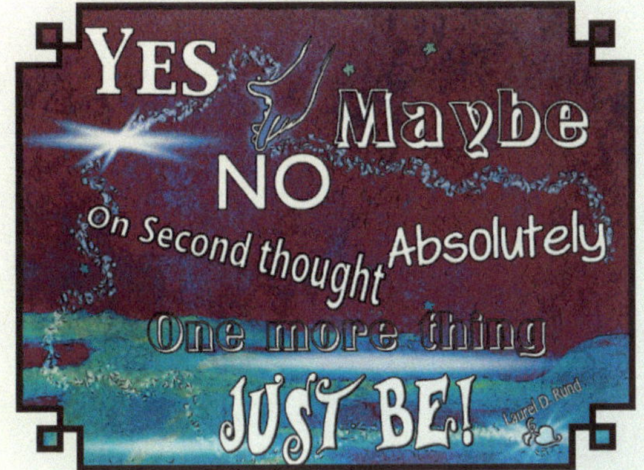

*A*fter listening to the "*story*" of my fears, a loving and wise sage said to me, *"Laurel, if you are afraid of losing your freedom, you are not truly free! **So my lady, JUST BE.**"* The wisdom of her words resonated with me and ***I got it!***

*I*t was then that I decided to let the relationship with my new friend form itself as it was meant to be. Today, this man whom I care deeply about has partnered with me in a caring and loving way. He honors my determination to be true to my "*essence*" and to be the courageous woman who emerged after a storm of loss and grief. I value, encourage and understand that he, too, needs to be true to his quintessential self.

*S*omehow through a mysterious force, we found one another at an unexpected time in our lives. Slowly, tentatively ~ but with intention ~ the two of us shared our stories, telling each other what lies beneath our outer facades, revealing feelings, fears, hopes and dreams. All of this has built a bridge of understanding and history between us. Whether by fate or by plan, an unexpected synchronistic encounter offered each of us a healing balm ~ the gift of love and renewal.

I thought I would be invisible after my husband's death. What I didn't realize was that I just had to look into the mirror and "***SEE***" me**!**

*R*omance in my 60's has given me much to be grateful for. Time compresses, wisdom from within is recognized and called upon, and most importantly ~ I have learned to **"Just Be."**

The rest has been falling into place one day, one hour, one minute at a time.

Laurel

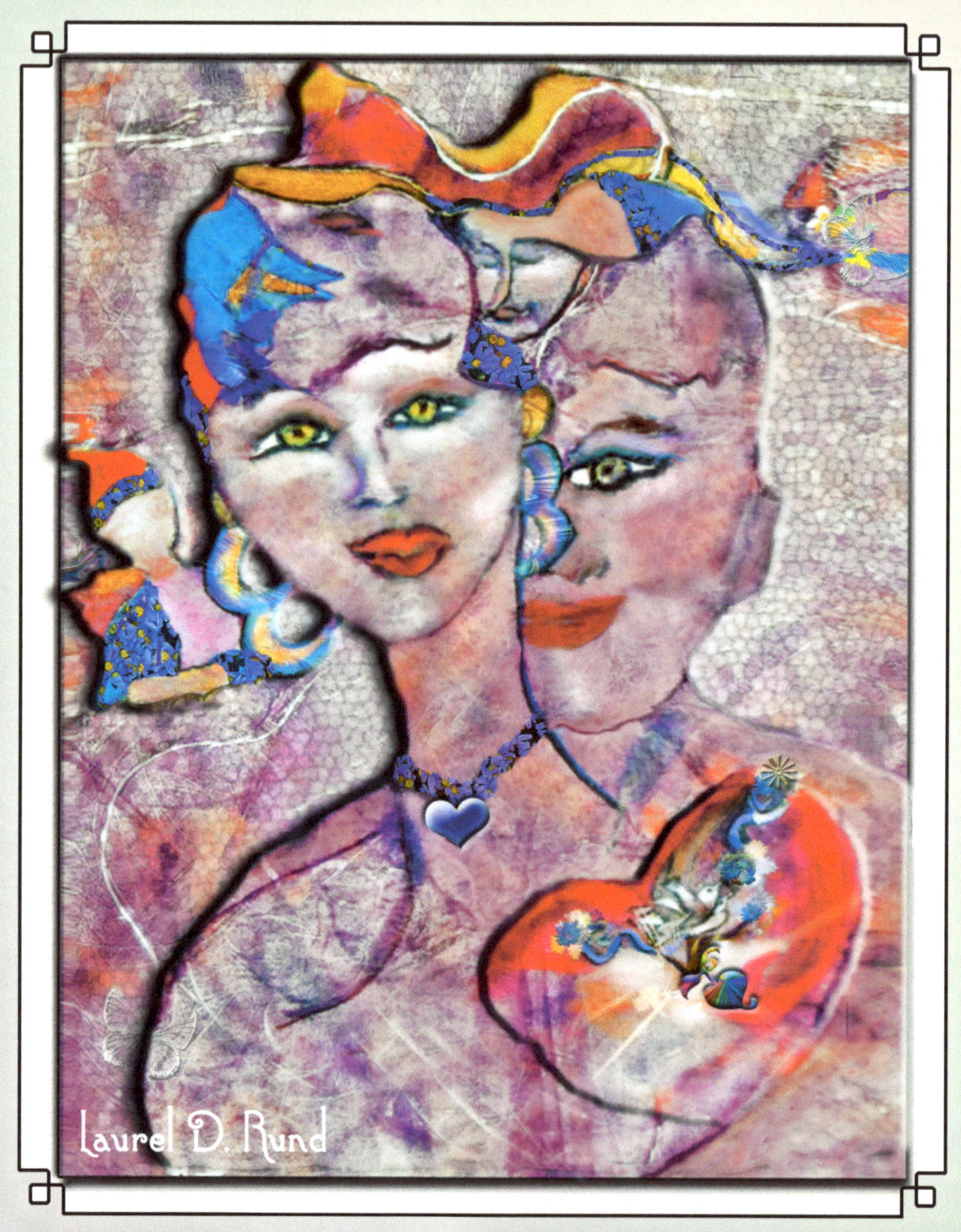

The Lovers

Can We ~ Will We?

You have entered my life at an unexpected time
and in the most unusual way.
Can we be separate and together and yet separate at the same time?
Will we mirror back tenderness and belief to one another?
Can I give myself to you without losing me?

Will we love each other with a warm and understanding heart?
Can we be quiet and trusting with each other?
Will your embrace be filled with the strength and tenderness I so desire?
When I lean back into your arms, can we 'just be'?

If I let you into my world and want you stay,
will you understand my desire to take wing and fly?
Will you cup my heart in your hands and be my nesting place?
Can we love one another while
dancing to the rhythm of our souls?

Will we play like butterflies, flitting over a
flower-filled meadow, tasting each other's nectar?
Can we jump into a waterfall and experience its delight?
Will our relationship be filled with hope and
the colors of a rainbow?

On this journey called life,
were we supposed to meet and share our hearts?
Can I rest safely in your arms as we breathe together and apart?
Has our soul story just begun?
Will you make my heart sing?

Laurel

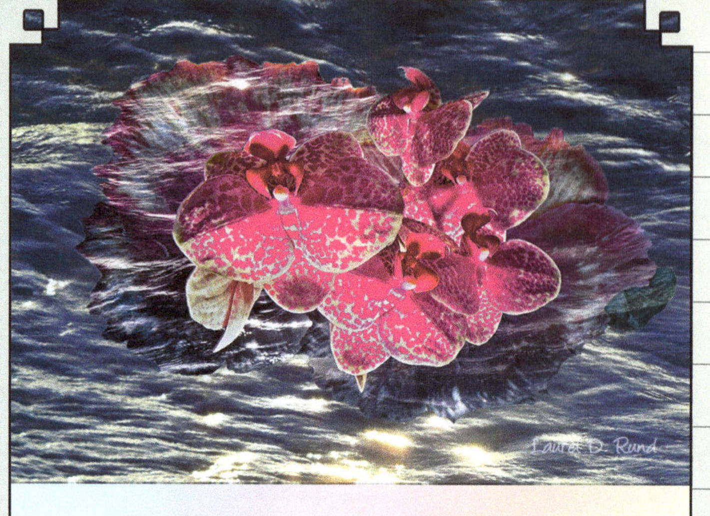

MOVING FORWARD

Laurel D. Rund

Let go of the past
and go for the future.
Go confidently in the direction
of your dreams.
Live the life you imagined!

Henry David Thoreau

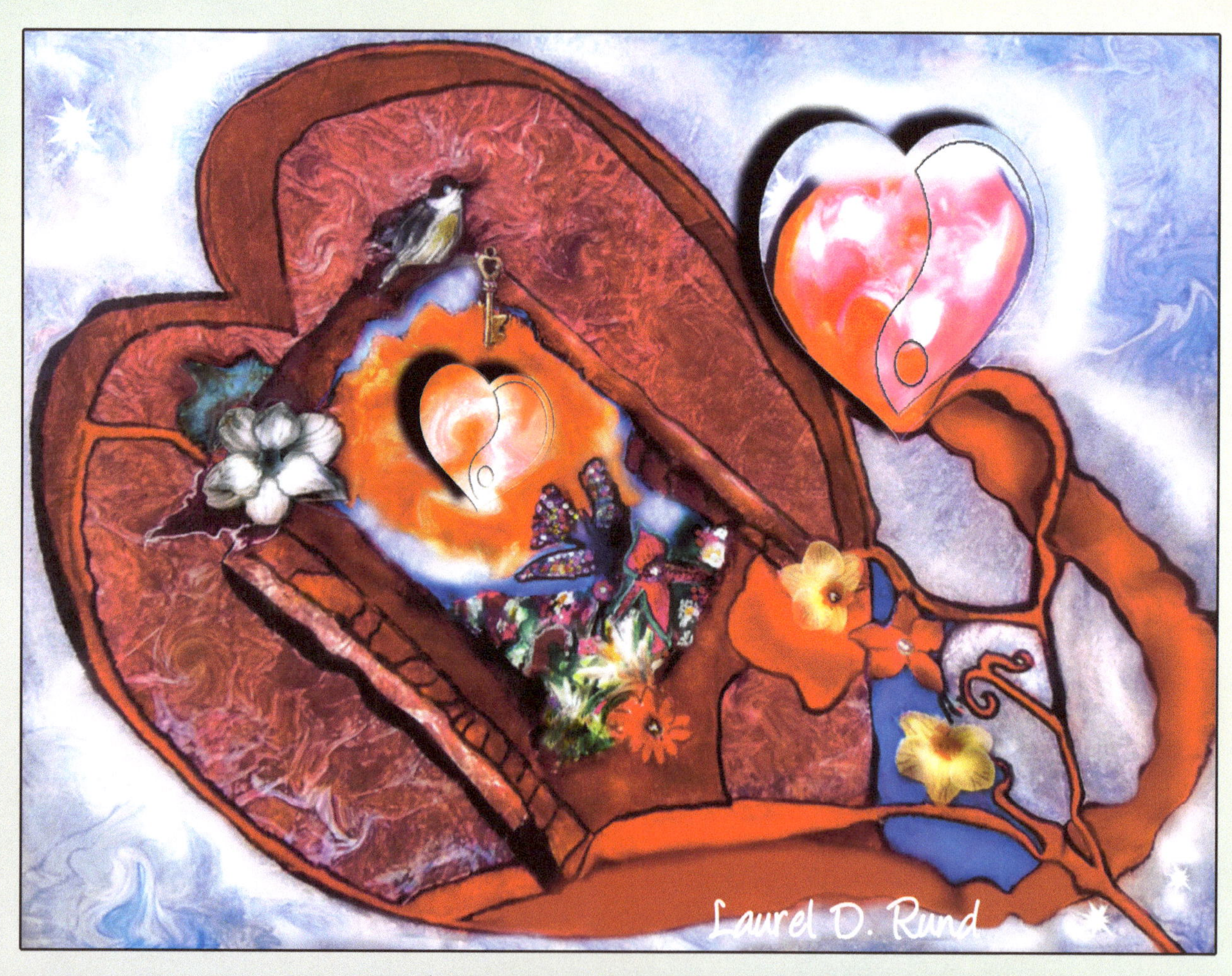

Come Home

Come Home

I listened to a voice from within which beckoned me to
come home, come home ~ open the doors to your heart.
So I closed my eyes, quieted my mind and asked
the twinkling stars to light the way.
My senses came alive ~ were heightened
when its crimson color and radiant glow came into view.

A door with glittering handles opened easily to my touch,
revealing sunlit clouds and a bright blue sky.
As I strolled through this enchanted place,
the most magnificent sounds and sights greeted me.

I knew I had found my Garden of Eden, my Nirvana,
when I heard my heart whisper tenderly to me …
Finally, finally you are here!
Welcome home, welcome home ~ welcome to your heart!

So, if you hear an Emerging Voice inviting you
to take a journey into your heart ~
go there, open its doors and discover
the treasures that lie within.
You will know you have found your way
when you hear these words ...
Finally, finally you are here!
Welcome home, welcome home ~ welcome to your heart!

Laurel

What People Are Saying

After the death of her husband, Laurel embraced the deep grief that followed and, in doing so, emerged with a strong and powerful voice that shows us the path towards growth and healing. Her artwork and poetry are an incredible testimony to the transformation that can take place when our hearts are open. My life has been enriched by the authentic message in Laurel's work. Yours will be too! *Jane Ogden*

These pieces have compelled me to look inside myself, even when I wanted to hide. Surprisingly, I found a strength I didn't know I had and am grateful for that gift. *Maureen Smith*

Laurel's beautiful writings and impassioned artwork are a feast for the heart and soul. They have inspired me to collaborate with her to create new music that captures the essence of her joy and love for life. One cannot help but be moved by the deep expressions of this very special woman. Laurel's artistic gifts are a treasure of refined gold. *Philip Wesley Leber*

Laurel's amazing artwork and heartfelt poems have reached that sheltered part of my soul, which allows me to get in touch with my own vulnerability and feel safe in its presence; but of utmost importance, provides me with Divine Permission to BE the woman that I AM! *Louise Aveni*

Laurel is a gifted artist and poet. Through her unique style, she has an amazing ability to express a journey of life's realities through her writing and artwork. The images created from fantastic colors and shapes relate a message from her heart and soul. Her words richly compliment her artwork and touch one's inner being. I love her and I love her inspired work. *Hannah Bellaff*

Laurel's words are as pleasing and as soft as the hand she lends. She has reminded me that grief is not something to fear, for it means I am lucky enough to be in love and to have loved. She has reminded me to never forget the blessings of the past but to always look to the future. For all of this, she has my love and gratitude. *Iris Frank*

Laurel's work is inspiring ~ as was witnessing how much she emerged after her deep grief. It gives me courage and hope to remember that out of the worst times can come creativity and growth! *Nancy Rubin*

Spirited and insightful, Laurel reaches deep inside and examines the feelings and emotions through her creative voice. Talented and generous, she shares these soulful visions through her artwork and poetry. Connecting with Laurel and her work has touched me and enhanced my life profoundly. *Susan Needle Vitale*

I have been deeply touched by the beautiful way Laurel expresses her feelings through her artwork and poems. Each creation is inspirational. *Rev. Sophie Bierker*

Laurel's poetry, writing and powerful energy take the place of life's superficial aspects with deep, sensitive, intelligent, bleeding thoughts of life, love and loss. She has put the beauty in life through her work and, moreover, through the sharing of her feelings and the giving of herself in helping others experience the reality of healing. *Melissa Rangell*

Laurel's heartfelt poetry speaks directly to my soul as it enriches and nurtures my own creative spirit. The original artwork accompanying her words adds another layer of meaning and is a delight for the eyes. *Madelaine Ginsberg*

Reading Laurel's poetry is like having a magical, mystical encounter with your heart. It's a transcendental experience and a beautiful celebration of the human spirit. *Linda Commito*

Laurel's grief was the catalyst for the creation of magic. Through her art and poetry we learn that even the deepest, darkest places within us can be accessible, ultimately beautiful and perhaps not as frightening as we thought. *Linda Maree*

I learned to love grief through Laurel's works. *Rev. Duffy Rutledge*

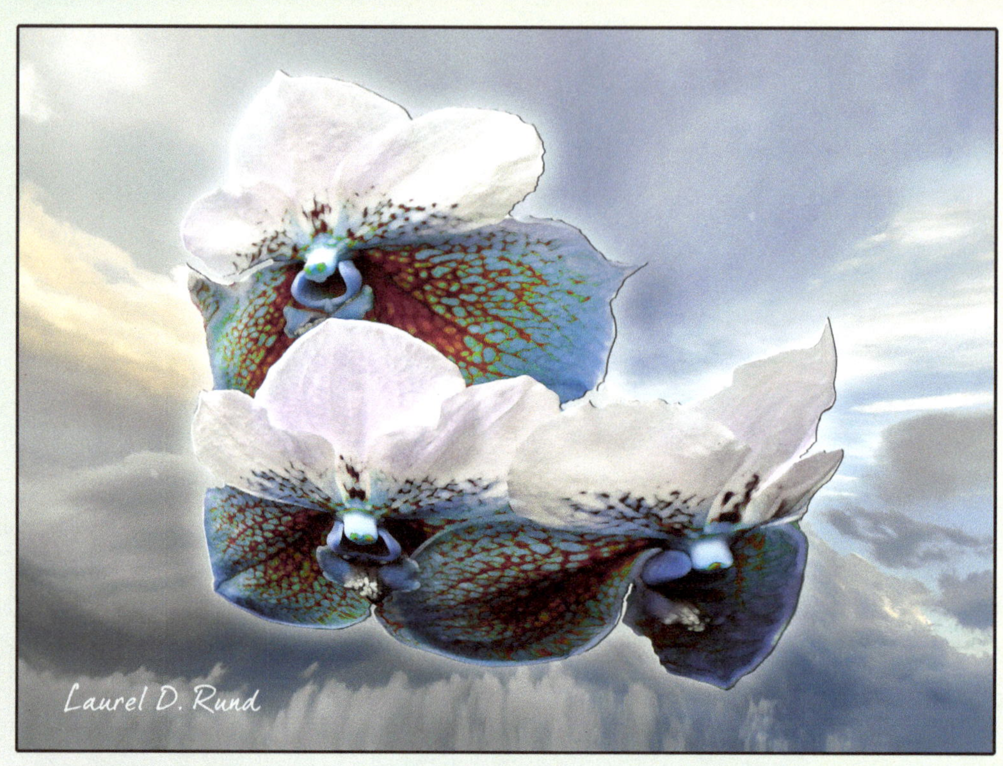

Fleur de Celeste

There is an unseen life that dreams us.
It knows our true direction and destiny.
We can trust ourselves more than we realize and
we need have no fear of change.

John O'Donohue

Art from the Heart

Inspirational Artist & Author

Laurel D. Rund

Essence of Laurel's

Art from the Heart

WEB: ESSENCEOFLAUREL.COM

EMAIL: ESSENCEOFLAUREL@ME.COM

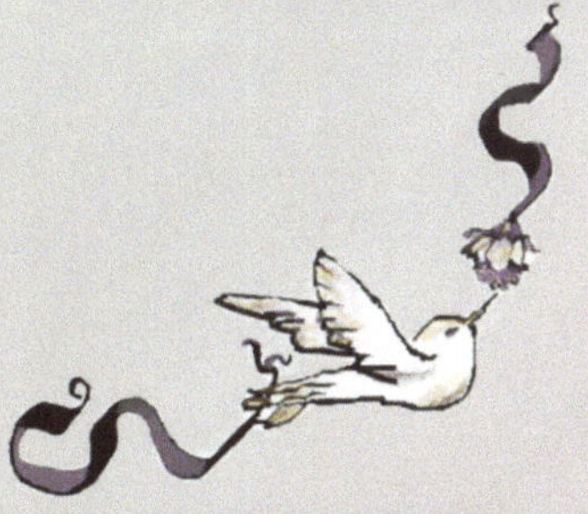

www.ingramcontent.com/pod-product-compliance
Lightning Source LLC
LaVergne TN
LVHW070143110826
845147LV00002B/317
9780615394305